BOXER

the Ferrari flat-12 racing and GT cars

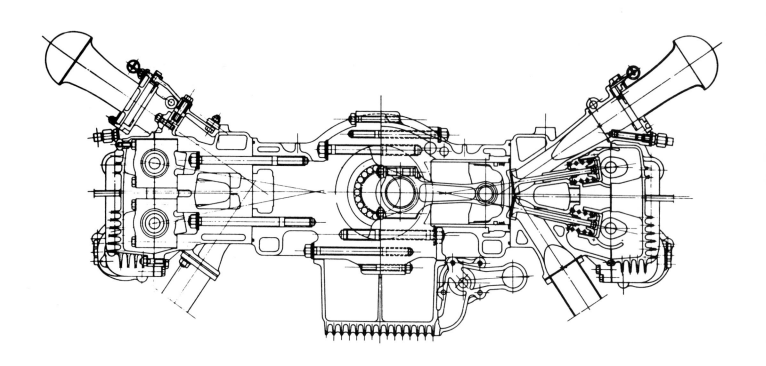

BOXER

the Ferrari flat-12 racing and GT cars

Jonathan Thompson

BOXER

the Ferrari flat-12 racing and GT cars

For Lesley and Kevin

Copyright 1981 © by the Newport Press and Osprey Publishing Limited

Printed in the United States of America.

ISBN 0-930880-05-6   The Newport Press
                      1001 West 18th Street
                      Costa Mesa, California 92627

ISBN 0-85045-409-3   Osprey Publishing Limited
                      12-14 Long Acre
                      London WC2E 9LP

Library of Congress card number 81-81133

U.S. distribution by:

Osceola, Wisconsin 54020, USA

Contents

Introduction

FERRARI CERTAINLY DID NOT invent the boxer engine. The horizontally-opposed configuration, with pistons punching side-to-side, has long been used in aircraft and motorcycles, usually air-cooled, and a number of production cars including the Volkswagen, Porsche, Lancia and Corvair applications.

Porsche, of course, was the foremost exponent of the horizontally-opposed engine in racing, with flat four, six, eight, twelve and even sixteen-cylinder units, all air-cooled, and the 911/935 series of sixes must be regarded as one of the most successful in the history of competition.

The first flat-12 Grand Prix engine was the 1.5-liter Tipo 512 produced by Alfa Romeo in 1939. Supercharged, it put out 335 bhp at 8600 rpm and was mounted at the rear of a chassis that, for all its technical interest, was not considered to be worth postwar development, and the 512 never raced. (Interestingly, the same designation was used by Ferrari for his first flat-12 Grand Prix car in 1964.) Alfa's next flat-12 was the Tipo 160, a 2.5-liter engine developed during 1952-54; like its predecessor, it was not destined to see competition. The chassis, a novel four-wheel-drive design with the engine and transaxle in front, was not constructed but the engine produced 285 bhp at 10,000 rpm and certainly would have been competitive in the 1954-1960 2.5-liter formula.

Cisitalia built the famous Porsche-designed Tipo 360 Grand Prix car in 1948, but the under-financed project was also abortive. Like the Alfa Romeo 512, it was a rear-engine supercharged 1.5-liter car; its output was 296 bhp at 8500 rpm and its chassis might be described as updated Auto Union. An attempt was made to continue the project in Argentina as the Autoar, but the single machine never raced and its greatest glory has been as a Porsche museum exhibit.

At the time that Ing. Mauro Forghieri began development of the boxer engine in 1963, no flat-12 car had yet raced and the honor fell to the blue and white Ferrari 512 F1 of Lorenzo Bandini at Watkins Glen in October 1964.

The next boxer engine could be considered to be the BRM H-16, in effect two flat-eights one above the other; designed for the 1966 3-liter formula, it was unsuccessful in the factory's own chassis but won one race in the back of a Lotus. The fabulous Porsche 917, with an air-cooled flat-12 that put out 520-665 bhp in 4.5/5.4-liter form and 1020 bhp as a turbocharged Can-Am unit, dominated Group 4, 5 and 7 racing during 1969-73. It was a diabolical machine to drive on all but the straightest courses, testing the genius of even such masters as Pedro Rodriguez and Josef Siffert, and the nimble 3-liter Ferrari 312 PB was a faster car on many circuits.

Alfa Romeo and Tecno also produced 3-liter flat-12 cars in the Seventies. Alfa's Tipo 33/12 sports car was reasonably competitive from the start and won the 1975 World Championship of Makes against reduced competition. Its engine was used by the Brabham team in Formula 1, before the components were redesigned in V-12 configuration to allow a chassis with better ground effect. Tecno's PA 123 Formula 1 car ran unsuccessfully in 1972-73; during the latter year its unreliable engine produced 470 bhp, compared to 485 for the Ferrari 312 B3 at that time.

Although it may have reached a temporary end to its career as a racing engine, the boxer configuration has served Ferrari well. In the 312 B through 312 T4 it won thirty-seven World Championship Formula 1 races, more than any other type of Ferrari engine,

"Ma con dodici cilindri—!" *Forghieri with Ferrari during 158 test, Monza, August 1963.*

The Fiorano circuit.

TV monitors for Fiorano circuit.

and six non-championship F1 events. In the 312 PB sports car it won twelve championship and three non-championship races, while the 2-liter 212 E won all nine of the hillclimbs it contested. Boxers have taken nine titles: the 1969 European Mountain Championship, the 1972 Sports Car World Championship, the 1975, 1977 and 1979 Drivers World Championships and the 1975, 1976, 1977 and 1979 Constructors World Championships. This is a record that speaks for itself; no other team has been in the forefront of world racing so consistently. The man responsible for the design of the boxer, Ing. Forghieri, must rank with the greatest racing engineers of all time.

This book project started over four years ago, at the time that Niki Lauda was winning his second World Championship, and the Ferrari boxer engine still had three more years of active competition. By bringing the story through the end of 1980, with a few Berlinetta Boxer highlights from 1981, we have been able to present a complete story of a very significant era in Ferrari technology, one that appears to be replaced by the new turbo era at Maranello. *BOXER* has taken a long time to compile, and the writer would like to thank the publisher Rich McCormack and the many contributors for their patience and assistance. Those who have provided material are credited in the Acknowledgements on page 184, but I would like to give special thanks to Peter Coltrin, Harley Cluxton, Geoff Goddard, Mike and Wilhelmina Sheehan, Dean Batchelor, Jean-Francois Marchet, Gerald Roush, Bob Tronolone and Chuck Queener, all of whose contributions, encouragement and assistance have been tremendously important.

Norwell, Mass. May 1981   Jonathan Thompson

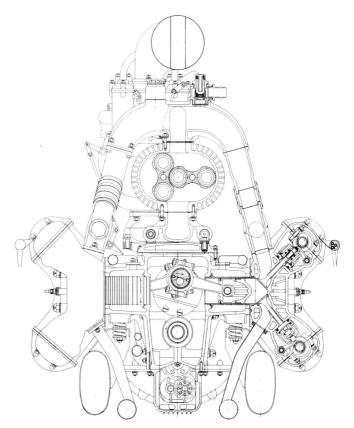

Alfa Romeo Tipo 512

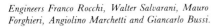
Engineers Franco Rocchi, Walter Salvarani, Mauro Forghieri, Angiolino Marchetti and Giancarlo Bussi.

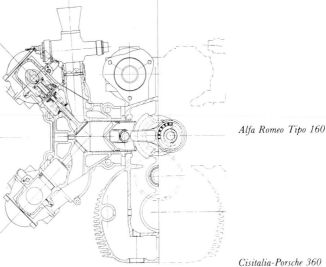

Alfa Romeo Tipo 160

Cisitalia-Porsche 360

Chapter 1

$512\,F1$ **Boxer Without Punch**

ERRARI'S FIRST ENGINES, the 125 S and 125 F1 of 1946-49, had been 1.5-liter twelves, in 60-degree V configuration. They were moderately successful, but the supercharged Formula 1 version only won races in the absence of the more fully developed Alfa Romeo 158 straight-eights, which dominated postwar Grand Prix racing. To beat Alfa, Ferrari engineer Aurelio Lampredi thus designed the 4.5-liter 375 F1 in 1950. Fourteen years would pass before Ferrari again ran a 1.5-liter twelve.

At the annual winter press conference in December 1963, Ferrari presented two engines for the 1964 season. One was the 158 F1, a V-8 which had been seen briefly at Monza the previous September in a semi-monocoque chassis designed especially for it. The second engine was a complete surprise—a 1.5-liter flat-12, with the cylinders horizontally opposed and punching side-to-side boxer fashion.

The horizontally-opposed engine layout was far from new—some of the background is discussed in the Introduction to this book—but this was the first boxer twelve actually destined for competition. Ferrari showed one assembled engine to the visiting journalists. It did not appear to have been run and the design was apparently just beginning its development program. No internal details were revealed, not even the bore and stroke dimensions, and it is probable these were dependent on further testing. In fact, the development period lasted another nine months until September 1964, when the first flat-12 powered car made its debut at Monza for the Italian Grand Prix.

In the meantime, the motoring press had only the external appearance of the one engine by which to judge its potential. It was reasonably compact, with a low center of gravity, even though the alternator, fuel pump and two fuel-injection pumps were stacked on top for accessibility and to minimize overall length. These accessories were driven from the back of the right intake camshaft by internally-cogged belts. The four overhead camshafts, operating one intake and one exhaust valve per cylinder, were gear-driven from the front of the crankshaft, while the twin distributors were chain-driven from this gear train. There was only one spark plug per cylinder, in contrast to Ferrari's usual practice of twin ignition on Formula 1 engines. The fuel injection system was Lucas indirect, with short intake tubes and the injectors close to the ports. The crankcase/cylinder block halves were cast in aluminum alloy, and presumably there were cast-iron cylinder liners and a seven-main-bearing crankshaft. Initially, the new engine was designated the 1512 F1 (for 1.5-liter, 12-cylinder For-

mula 1). Ferrari has shortened this to 512 F1 and the latter designation is used in this book.

Ferrari has never promoted personalities within his staff, but the 512 F1 was basically the work of Mauro Forghieri, a young engineer who had worked on the 250 GTO program during 1962-63 and who was to become, with occasional fluctuations in favor dictated by current fortunes, the chief design engineer in the racing department.

Before the competition appearance of the 512 F1, the 1964 Grand Prix battle was waged effectively if not brilliantly by the 158 F1 and the older 156 F1; the engine of the latter was a V-6 dating back to 1961. Driving the V-8, John Surtees had achieved a second place at Zandvoort, a third at Brands Hatch, and had won the German Grand Prix at the Nürburgring for the second year in a row. His teammate Lorenzo Bandini had used a V-8 in some races but his points (from a fifth at Brands Hatch, a third at the Nürburgring and a victory at Zeltweg) were scored with the V-6 car. Ferrari's major rivals were Jim Clark in the Lotus 33 and Dan Gurney in the Brabham BT11 (both using the Coventry Climax FWMV V-8, which produced 204 bhp at 9500 rpm), and Graham Hill in the BRM T261, which had its own V-8 putting out just over 200 bhp at 10,500 rpm. Against these, the 158 F1 delivered 205 bhp at 11,000 rpm and the 156 F1 gave 195-200 bhp at 10,200. In handling, there was little to choose between the British and Italian cars, the new semi-monocoque Ferrari chassis bringing it up to the mark in this department, but when Clark's Lotus was performing properly, his driving gave him the edge.

Ferrari had scored two victories in succession going into the Italian Grand Prix, and for this race brought five cars: two V-8s for Surtees to choose from, a V-6 each for Bandini and Lodovico Scarfiotti, and at long last, a flat-12. The 512 F1 had a chassis almost identical to the 158 F1, with a 20-mm increase in wheelbase (from 2380 to 2400) and three liters more fuel capacity (128 vs. 125 for the V-8). With its engine cover in place, the 512 F1 was only distinguishable by the twelve intake trumpets showing through the protective wire screening, and one had to look closely to see that there were six exhaust pipes coming out each side instead of four.

The engine itself was noticeably changed from the first flat-12 shown to the press nine months before. The entire fuel injection system was reworked using Bosch components (as on the 158 F1), with the intake tubes much longer and angled inward, and the injectors further away from the ports. Bosch ignition

Ferrari's first boxer engine, the 512 F1,
was shown to the press in December 1963.

Public debut for 512 F1 was at Monza 1964;
Lorenzo Bandini practiced but did not race it.

Cooling problems called for supplementary
radiator in first race at Watkins Glen.

Flat-12 engine fit on 158 F1 chassis as
though designed for it; wheelbase was longer.

9

Graham Hill's BRM tangled with Bandini at Mexico City, giving championship to Surtees.

For 1965 the 512 F1 engine had twin plugs and 225 bhp. At Monte Carlo, Bandini (leading Surtees' 158 F1) scored a second place, the 512 F1's best performance.

Extra fuel tank above engine was required for ultra-fast Spa-Francorchamps circuit.

Surtees won the Nurburgring with V-6 in 1963 and V-8 in 1964 but could not score the hat-trick with flat-12 in 1965.

Surtees qualified fifth and finished third in his first race with 512 F1 at Silverstone.

was also used, and there were four coils mounted high at the back of the engine. The bore and stroke dimensions finally chosen were 56 x 50.4 mm, giving a single-cylinder capacity of 124.13 cc (close to the 125 figure which had provided the designation for the very first Ferraris) and a total displacement of 1489.63 cc. The power output was probably about 210-215 bhp at 11,500 rpm, with a compression ratio of 9.8:1. For the improved 512 F1 used at Mexico City at the end of the season, with revised camshafts and injectors closer to the ports, the output was quoted as 220 bhp.

Bandini drove the 512 F1 in practice on the day before the Italian Grand Prix, but he did not reach any really competitive times because of the weather.

For this reason, and probably because Ferrari did not want to give the still unsorted car its debut in front of the Italian public, the 512 F1 was withdrawn. Bandini was naturally disappointed, but took over Surtees' spare 158 F1 for the race. The event was a complete triumph for Surtees, who qualified on the pole, led most of the race, set the fastest lap and won by over a minute. Bandini drove a good race, just beating Richie Ginther's BRM into third place at the finish.

With three wins in a row, Ferrari was now fully competitive in Formula 1 for the first time since 1961, and Surtees was a strong contender for World Champion. Now came a strange development which caused the championship-winning car to be painted

11

blue and white rather than red. Ferrari had sought to homologate the 250 LM as a GT car, but this was blocked by the *Federation Internationale de l'Automobile,* the FIA stating that the handful of 250 LMs produced was insufficient for the category (nominally 100 units, but often freely interpreted in the past). Enzo Ferrari felt that the *Automobile Club d'Italia,* the Italian member of the FIA, had not worked fully in his behalf. He was so enraged that he renounced his membership in the ACI and entered his Grand Prix cars under the aegis of the North American Racing Team (Ferrari's U.S. distributor, managed by Luigi Chinetti). The cars were repainted blue and white for the last two 1964 races at Watkins Glen, New York and Mexico City. NART's rectangular emblem even replaced the Scuderia Ferrari shield on the sides of the cars.

American Racing Debut

So THE 512 F1 made its actual racing debut in American colors. As the V-8 car was considered more reliable for Surtees' Championship prospects, Bandini was given the flat-12 for Watkins Glen. He qualified the car eighth on the grid and retired with engine trouble after 58 of the 110 laps; his highest position during the race was fifth. Surtees, on the other hand, kept his hopes alive by qualifying his V-8 second (to Clark) and finishing in the same position (behind Hill). This meant that he had 34 Championship points going into the last event at Mexico City, compared to a scorable 39 for Hill. Clark, with 30 points, could win the title with a victory if Hill was pointless in Mexico and Surtees third or worse. The Ferrari driver needed either a first or a second to beat Hill, so there were many possible permutations.

In the race, it was the 512 F1 which was the determining factor, although not in the most glorious fashion. Ferrari entered three completely different cars for the Mexican event: the usual V-8 for Surtees, a V-6 for local driver Pedro Rodriguez, and a flat-12 for Bandini. Being a Ferrari mechanic was obviously not as simple a job as some others! The 512 F1 had several engine modifications, including new camshaft profiles and revised injection tubes. The changes were effective, giving at least 5 bhp more and allowing Bandini to qualify the car third, one-tenth of a second faster than his team leader's 158 F1.

Clark led easily from Gurney, with Bandini pushing Hill for third position. On lap 31 came the most significant moment of the race, one that determined the final Championship standings after ten hard races. Hill had been using a lot of track trying to keep ahead of the Italian, who dogged him relentlessly. On the tight hairpin turn on the back side of the course, Hill went very wide and Bandini tried to drive through the opening. Hill reacted by tightening his turn, the cars touched, and the BRM went off the track. This spoiled Hill's title chances, but the advantage to Ferrari was not immediately realized.

Clark still led the race, and looked like a certain Champion.

But two laps from the end the oil pressure in Clark's Climax V-8 went to zero and he pulled out of the race. This gave Gurney the lead with Bandini second and Surtees now third. Ferrari's team manager Franco Lini realized that Surtees could win the Championship by one point by finishing second, so Bandini was signaled to fall back behind his teammate. This done, Surtees and the Ferrari 158 F1 were World Champions.

The 512 F1 had performed well and Bandini, though criticized by those who favored Graham Hill for Champion, had driven an excellent race. Rodriguez placed the 156 F1 sixth, so the three diverse Ferrari entries all finished in the points. A satisfactory result, if not entirely expected, for the Italian team.

1965 Anti-Climax

THE FOLLOWING YEAR, the last of the 1.5-liter Formula 1, was an anti-climax for Ferrari. The cars were painted red again, as everyone familiar with the Italian temperament expected, but the promise of the Boxer twelve was not fulfilled. Despite further development, which included twin ignition and a final output of 225 bhp, the 512 F1 did not win a single race. Its performance was comparable to that of the 158 F1 during the first part of the season and only by the middle of the year was its margin sufficient for Surtees to choose it over his customary V-8.

In South Africa, Bandini broke down with electrical failure after completing 66 laps. In the non-championship races at Siracusa and Silverstone, he placed the 512 F1 third and seventh, the engine running very roughly in the British race. The 512 F1's best result came at Monte Carlo, where Bandini qualified it fourth, just ahead of Surtees' V-8, and drove to second place behind an uncatchable Graham Hill, the longtime master of the Monaco circuit. The 512 F1 looked different at Monte Carlo, with about 20 cm of its nose trimmed away to minimize the chances of cooling loss through collision damage; this was a normal modification for many cars which raced on the tight, twisty circuit.

For the Belgian Grand Prix at Spa-Francorchamps, where continued high-speed driving resulted in higher fuel consumption, both Bandini's 512 F1 and Surtees' 158 F1 had supplementary tanks, of approximately 10 liters, mounted above their engines. But neither car was competitive and Bandini worked his way up to a ninth-place finish after starting fifteenth. He qualified on the front row in France, however, third fastest behind Clark's Lotus and Jackie Stewart's BRM, but knocked off a wheel on lap 37 and retired.

Surtees took over the flat-12 for the next three races but fared no better. He was never higher than third in the British Grand Prix and finished seventh,

a lap behind, in the Dutch race. Trying for a third successive victory at the Nürburgring , Surtees had two 512 F1s at his disposal. He qualified on the outside of the front row but was over five seconds slower than Clark, who walked off with the race. Surtees had gear-selector troubles on the first lap and retired after 11 laps when in last place. The flat-12 had not been able to complete the hat-trick started by the V-6 and V-8 Ferraris.

In an attempt to restore prestige in their home race at Monza, Ferrari designed new cylinder heads, revised the injection trumpets and produced two 512 F1s for Surtees and Bandini. The British driver qualified for the center of the front row, between Clark and Stewart, and Bandini was fifth fastest, on the second row. A slipping clutch dropped Surtees to the middle of the pack on the first lap but he actually worked his way back into the lead (on lap 15) before retiring on the 35th lap. Bandini had a steady race into fourth place.

Out With a Whimper

AFTER "BIG JOHN" had a serious accident in a sports car race in Canada, his place in the second 512 F1 was taken by Rodriguez. Neither Bandini nor the Mexican was competitive in the U.S. race, in which they finished fourth and fifth respectively. The last race of the year, and the final event of the five-year 1.5-liter Formula 1, was the Mexican Grand Prix, for which Ferrari entered three twelves, the third one for Scarfiotti. Only two of them started, Rodriguez taking over Scarfiotti's car after crashing his own in practice. This year the Ferraris lacked power on the high-altitude circuit, and Rodriguez and Bandini were seventh and eighth, three laps behind Ginther's winning Honda V-12, which had the distinction of scoring Goodyear's first Formula 1 victory.

The 512 F1 went out with a whimper. The expected power had been realized at maximum revolutions, but the torque curve was never broad enough to make the car superior on any circuit. Was the flat-12 engine a dead end? For the time being, the answer was yes, as Ferrari reverted to the classic V-12 layout for the 3-liter Formula 1 beginning in 1966. But an experimental sports/racing car was to further the potential of the flat-12 configuration and lead to an entirely new series of Formula 1 boxers for the 1970s.

13

Chapter 2

212 E Montagna Unchallenged Champion

THE 512 F1 FERRARI flat-12 raced during 1964-65 showed only occasional—and marginal—improvement over the V-8 powered 158 F1 cars, and neither engine type gave Ferrari a victory in the final year of the 1.5-liter Formula 1. For the new 3-liter formula that began in 1966, Maranello returned to the traditional V-12 layout, one that had brought the company hundreds of victories in Grand Prix and sports car competition. It seemed that the flat-12 engine had been an unproductive venture.

For over two years nothing was heard of the flat-12 layout, until a car known as the Sport 2000 was tested at the Modena aerodrome circuit by Chris Amon in 1967. The Sport 2000 looked just like a V-6 sport/racing Dino spyder, and in fact had the chassis of the Dino 206 S used by Lodovico Scarfiotti in the 1967 Trento-Bondone hillclimb. This car differed externally only in the absence of air intakes from the center of the rear deck, but underneath was a new engine, a 2-liter flat-12.

This second-generation flat-12 was developed by Ing. Stefano Jacoponi from Forghieri's original 1.5-liter design. Despite a 33-percent increase in displacement, the 2-liter was far more compact, having only four main bearings, a much narrower arrangement of the 48 valves, with an included angle of only 27 degrees, and lower-mounted ignition and fuel-injection components. The bore and stroke dimensions were more oversquare at 65 x 50 mm. The enlargement of the bore provided for the overall displacement increase to 1990.98 cc, while the stroke was a fraction shorter than on the 1.5-liter unit. Lucas indirect fuel injection was used, but with intake ports at an angle of approximately 45 degrees (compared to nearly vertical pipes on the 512 F1), and the compression ratio was 11.0:1.

As originally tested the Sport 2000 produced a healthy 290 bhp at 11,800 rpm. This gave a specific output of 145.6 bhp/liter, slightly less than on the 1965 Formula 1 car. The sports car scaled only 500 kg (just over 1100 pounds) complete, so the weight/power ratio was an impressively low 1.72 kg/bhp. Ferrari had a little bomb on their hands.

But what to do with it? Ferrari decided to avoid road racing and instead selected a different approach. Having just barely won the 1967 championship after a heavy onslaught from Ford, Chaparral and the ever more potent Porsche machines, Ferrari was disenchanted with sports car racing, especially the rules which favored 5-liter cars like the Ford GT-40, and 1968 was the first year in the firm's history that there were no works-entered Ferrari sports cars in international competition. The Dinos had been reasonably effective in the 2-liter class during 1966-1967 but naturally had not scored any major overall victories, and their development was discontinued. To replace them in the long-distance sports car events with the Sport 2000 would have been expensive and probably no more rewarding, as the new car was basically a sprint machine unlikely to last 1000 km.

Boxer engine of 212 E displaced 1991 cc and produced 290-295 bhp at 11,500 rpm; design was much more compact than 512 F1.

Using Dino 206 chassis, first flat-12 sports car was tested by Amon at Modena in November 1967, known unofficially as the Sport 2000.

Tests with 212 E in winter of 1968-69 by Amon (shown) and Schetty produced unbeatable hillclimb car for European Mountain Championship; note front and rear spoilers.

Ing. Stefano Jacoponi, here with car in May
1969, developed engine from Forghieri design.

17

However, the Sport 2000 was ideally suited for the European Mountain Championship, a series of eight hillclimbs for 2-seat racing cars with an upper displacement limit of 2 liters (as well as cars in the GT and Touring Car categories). Begun in 1957, this championship had been prestigious, especially for Porsche, which had won the title nine times. When Ferrari made a serious effort in this series, as they had in 1962 and 1965 with Scarfiotti, the title had been returned to Italy in convincing fashion. With Porsche dominant in all the intervening years, it seemed time for Ferrari to reassert themselves in this class, and a full program was planned for 1969.

Peter Schetty

INSTRUMENTAL IN THIS PROGRAM was a 27-year old Swiss driver named Peter Schetty, who had much hillclimb experience and was also a capable test driver. Driving a Ford Mustang, Schetty had placed second in the GT category in the 1966 championship, and in 1967 he was engaged by Abarth as their main development driver, as well as competing in the hillclimbs and other sports car events. That year he placed his Abarth 2000 an excellent third overall in the Mountain championship, behind the much faster Porsche 910s of Gerhard Mitter and Rolf Stommelen.

Employed by Ferrari, Schetty did almost all of the development testing of the Sport 2000 at Modena and Vallelunga. Now designated 212 E (2-liter, 12-cylinder, Europeo) and also known as the Montagna (mountain) car, the 212 E had gained another 10 bhp, for an even 300, by the beginning of 1969. The bodywork had been simplified (headlights were not necessary, minimal fuel tankage was required and the rear fenders were abbreviated) but weight was slightly increased. Minor aerodynamic changes were made (tabs on the front fenders, a more abrupt spoiler on the rear deck) but the chassis was still essentially Dino. The specialized nature of the exercise was emphasized by the fact that the longest distance the car would have to cover on any one run was 21.6 km (13.4 miles) and the durability of the components was not a major concern. On the other hand, complete engine rebuilds were not desirable, so water and oil temperatures had to be strictly controlled. For the former, there was a front-mounted radiator with an expansion tank; for the latter, a large reservoir, three pumps and a radiator above the engine with a large scoop on the rear deck. There was no brake cooling, a deliberate omission to ensure their rapid warm-up on the shortest courses.

By mid-season the 212 E was developing 315-320 bhp for brief periods, and a consistent 295 bhp at 11,500 rpm. Ferrari considered running the 212 E in the endurance races at Brands Hatch and the Nürbugring; it would have been more than competitive in speed, but unlikely to last the distance.

When the hillclimb season began, Ferrari found their main rival absent; Porsche no longer thought it desirable to contest the championship, being busy with the 3-liter 908 Prototypes in the international endurance races as well as with the development of the 4.5-liter flat-12 917 in the Sports category, for which 25 machines had to be constructed. It might be mentioned that Ferrari also had its 3-liter Prototype, the 312 P, had begun the design of a 5-liter Sports machine, the 512 S, was active in Formula 1 with the 312 F1 and partially committed in Group 7 with the 612/712 Can-Am! This excessive involvement in different categories of the sport severely limited Ferrari's effectiveness in all of them, a lesson Maranello was slow to learn. In the Forties, Fifties and mid-Sixties this rich variety had been possible, contributing to the Ferrari legend all over the world. But the increasing cost and specialization, resulting from and encouraging outside sponsorship, changed the nature of racing, away from the emphasis on sport and toward the realm of big business.

The immediate result of Porsche's absence from the mountain events was the instant and total domination of the Ferrari 212 E. The only other competitor in the 2-Seat Racing Car class was the Abarth 2000; with only 250-260 bhp it was not even a close challenger, and after two events the Torino firm concentrated on the Sport category, which it in turn could dominate.

A Run of Victories

FERRARI BEGAN A RUN of overall victories and absolute course records so predictable that even the specialist racing publications found them boring to report on, and the championship was largely ignored, except in end-of-season summaries. In addition to two climbs at Ampus and Volterra which were not part of the championship series, Schetty won seven title events for an unbroken run of nine straight victories in nine tries: Ampus, Volterra, Montseny, Rossfeld, Mont-Ventoux, Trento-Bondone, Freiburg-Schauinsland, Cesana-Sestriere and Ollon-Villars. As only the seven best of the eight performances counted for the championship standings, there was little point in Ferrari's contesting the final hillclimb at Gaisberg, Austria, where the financial inducement was also considered too small by the Italian team.

So Schetty's real job in 1969 was to break the course records, which he did by precise driving that occasionally bordered on the fantastic, and it was a shame that there was no major Porsche opposition to heighten the performances. The only course where Schetty failed to establish an absolute record was at Rossfeld, Germany, because of heavy fog, but he was nevertheless the fastest competitor by almost half a minute. At the conclusion of the season, the car was sold to Edoardo Lualdi Gabardi.

Four years before, the 512 F1 had failed to win a single race, but the 212 E was victorious every time the factory ran it. The Boxer engine was clearly on its way to better things.

Peter Schetty testing 212 E at Modena in 1969; note mounting of radiator scoop above engine, absence of headlights.

Schetty won nine out of nine hillclimbs contested in 1969, including Ollon-Villars.

Chapter 3

312 B F1 **Grand Prix Renaissance**

*View below 312 B shows compact exhausts,
extreme rear mounting of twin oil coolers.*

*Ickx gave 312 B its debut at Kyalami in March
1970; South African heat called for shortened nose.*

DURING THE LATE 1960s it seemed inevitable that
Chris Amon would win a World Championship
Formula 1 race, and that he would do it at the wheel
of a Ferrari. The young New Zealander spent three
seasons with the Italian team, usually competitive
and on several occasions tantalizingly close to success. But the single victory Ferrari achieved during
his tenure was scored by his teammate Jacky Ickx, in
the 1968 French Grand Prix at Rouen.

In the summer of 1969 the V-12 era was drawing
to a close for Ferrari. An entirely new engine was in
the works, one that would ultimately bring more Formula 1 victories than any previous Maranello design.
But Chris Amon's patience was exhausted. While he
might have seen the potential of the new 312 B, he
no longer had faith in Ferrari reliability, and an
engine blow-up in testing prior to the Italian Grand
Prix was the final straw. Amon packed his bags. Like
so many drivers, he had been on the Ferrari team at
the wrong time.

Ing. Mauro Forghieri's new 312 B engine, compact and disarmingly simple in appearance, brought
the boxer technology to full fruition, and an elegant
new chassis came with it, taking advantage of the
engine's lower center of gravity. While Pedro Rodriguez drove the old V-12 in the few remaining races of
1969, the new car's test program continued and
Jacky Ickx was offered a contract for the 1970 season.
To achieve the desired compactness—not an easy task
as the previous, bulky Alfa Romeo and Cisitalia
flat-12s had shown—Forghieri used only four main
bearings instead of the usual seven. Initially, with
roller bearings and built-up crankshafts, the engines
failed in testing, causing Amon's disillusionment.
Changing to machined one-piece crankshafts was an
improvement, but it took a special Pirelli-developed
rubber coupling between the crankshaft and flywheel
to move the major torsional stress away from a cri-
tical point on the crank and make it reliable. The
resulting engine has been remarkably strong during
its eleven-year racing career; except for lubrication
problems experienced in mid-1971, the 312 B has been
acknowledged the most consistently dependable unit
in Formula 1.

The boxer's bore and stroke dimensions were initially 78.5 x 51.5 mm, giving a displacement of 2991
cc. The aluminum-alloy crankcase/cylinder block was
in two halves, split vertically down the center, with
cast-iron liners. Abandoning his original idea for a
cogged rubber belt (which would have required extra
space) to drive the four overhead camshafts, Forghieri
utilitzed a train of gears at the output (rear) end of

In the writer's opinion the best-looking rear-engine Formula 1 car ever designed, the 312 B was first tested at Modena in September 1969. In group are Schetty, mechanic Borsari, Amon, engineers Bussi and Marelli (backs to camera), Forghieri (partly hidden) and Ferrari.

Hill's Lotus passes burned-out wreckage of Ickx' 312 B (foreground) and Oliver's BRM at Jarama. Ickx received moderate burns.

Ickx recovered to drive at Monte Carlo but a broken driveshaft joint put him out of the race.

Forghieri, center, watches as mechanic works on Ickx' engine before Belgian Grand Prix.

Ignazio Giunti drove second 312 B to fourth place in his debut at Spa-Francorchamps.

the engine. The camshafts operated two intake and two exhaust valves per cylinder; after experimenting with various valve layouts and finding no significant difference in the power outputs attainable, the designer selected an included angle of only 20 degrees, even smaller than on the 212 E, as offering the best possible combustion chamber. With such compactness, Ferrari's traditional use of twin ignition gave way to a single spark plug per cylinder. Lucas fuel injection was mounted above each bank of cylinders, and an elaborately curved set of four headers kept the exhaust system compatibly shallow with the engine's low build. A comparison of the cross sections of the 512 F1 and the 312 B F1 makes the reduction in height dramatically obvious. The weight of the 312 B was a satisfactory 145 kg (just under 320 lb). On an 11.8:1 compression ratio, the power output of the new 3-liter boxer was 455 bhp at 11,500 rpm, nearly 20 bhp higher than that of the final version of the V-12 and the rival Ford Cosworth DFV, but Forghieri was looking ahead to an eventual speed of at least 1000 rpm greater.

Conceived in parallel with the engine was a completely fresh chassis, with the same 312 B designation. In the writer's opinion, this chassis was the most handsome rear-engined Formula 1 design ever produced. By the most recent standards of low, angular monocoque design, the 312 B's slim contour and oval-section skinned tubular framework are decidedly passé, but at the close of the Sixties it set a new level of overall efficiency. Wings were still relatively new—and small— in Formula 1 at that time and the 312 B had a low-mounted main airfoil just ahead of the rear wheels. The driver was seated much farther to the rear than in late-Seventies practice, giving the 312 B a comparatively long nose. The semi-monocoque aluminum-skinned structure extended behind the driver and the engine was suspended below it. The nose piece, cockpit fairing and twin rear oil-cooler housings were formed of fiberglass. The complete car weighed just 534 kg (1177 lb)—this was before the FIA minimum of 575 was instituted— so the weight/power ratio was only 1.17 kg/bhp.

No great changes in transmission or suspension were incorporated in the original 312 B. The gearbox, a longitudinally-positioned 5-speed, was similar to that used with the V-12s. The suspension, in front by upper rocker arms, inboard coil spring/shock absorber units and wide-base lower A-arms, and at the rear by single upper links and reversed lower A-arms, had the basic layout of the earlier cars with the improvements in geometry resulting from the lower build. Firestone tires, used by Ferrari since mid-1966, were mounted, 13-inch in front and 15-inch in back. The main change at the rear was the outboard mounting of the disc brakes. This was a solution peculiar to the 312 B, resulting from the

Ickx was third in 1970 Dutch Grand Prix after starting from the front row and leading first lap.

wide engine and the position of the oil radiators; the 312 B2 and later Formula 1 boxers reverted to the usual inboard rear brakes, mounted on the differential.

A New Team

AFTER THE DISMAL 1969 SEASON and Amon's departure, the Italian press was happy to rumor and then confirm the signing of Ickx for 1970. The 25-year-old Belgian had won Ferrari's most recent Grand Prix victory and had enjoyed a fine 1969 season with Brabham, winning two more Grands Prix and becoming recognized as the most serious challenger to the World Champion, Jackie Stewart. At Ferrari, probably more than with any other team, emotional pressures can become so intense that a long period of failure can be overcome only by a complete reorganization of personnel and equipment. With an all-new car and a driver who was a proven winner, Ferrari put the first four years of the 3-liter Formula 1 behind them and once again took steady aim on Grand Prix dominance.

While the promise was obvious, the results were not immediate. For each of the first three races only a single entry was made for Ickx, although later drives, once the car was fully raceworthy, were planned for the Italian Ignazio Giunti and the Swiss Gianclaudio (Clay) Regazzoni. The debut of the 312 B came at Kyalami in South Africa on 7 March 1970; one car, chassis number 001, was taken to the circuit. Incorporating the internal engine improvements made over the winter, the car was externally almost the same as at its press debut six months before. Lighter, slim-spoked Campagnolo wheels replaced the star-pattern type used since mid-1966, the fire extinguisher was moved from the under side of the rollbar/wing brace to the front bulkhead, and there was a minor change to the lower rear of the chassis paneling, ahead of the engine. Two modifications made especially for the hot weather expected in South Africa were an additional oil tank mounted above the gearbox, between the twin cooling ducts, and a nose piece cut back about 10 cm to increase the area of the radiator air entry.

In the first two practice sessions Ickx was troubled by an engine that smoked badly and was decidedly down on power; when a new one was flown in and installed he improved his time to fifth fastest overall. In the race he ran second to Stewart for five laps, but running over a curb he fractured an oil line and was forced to retire after 60 laps with a seized engine.

Two chassis were available to Ickx for the next race, at Jarama in Spain, and he qualified 002 seventh, in the middle of the third row. But another incident, much more serious, occurred on the first lap, one that could have ended his career. Going into turn four, the BRM of Jackie Oliver lost its brakes and hit the 312 B amidships. The Ferrari's fuel tanks were punctured and both cars were instantly aflame;

Oliver freed himself immediately but Ickx could not have got out without the courageous assistance of a Spanish soldier working as a course marshal. Burned on the hands and thighs, Ickx also suffered gasoline burns from his soaked driving suit.

Although not entirely healed, Ickx recovered sufficiently to make the Monte Carlo race three weeks later. Qualifying fifth in chassis 001, he had a new car as a back-up, 003 replacing the car burnt out in Spain. He ran fifth at Monaco until a driveshaft universal joint failed on lap 12. The Ferrari had not finished a race so far in the season, but the performances were encouraging. With a new 002 built, there were three chassis available and Giunti made

312 B (Ickx) and Matra (Beltoise) led French Grand Prix but Jochen Rindt's Lotus won it.

his Ferrari debut as teammate to Ickx at Spa-Francorchamps in Belgium. Qualifying eighth, the Italian drove a steady race into fourth place, scoring the 312 B's first championship points. Ickx started fourth on the grid but his term of trial was not over; this time a loose fuel line leaked into the cockpit and aggravated his recent skin burns. Yet he drove into eighth place, only one lap down after a pit stop to refuel the car and pour water down his back to relieve the pain.

His first concrete results came in the Dutch Grand Prix at Zandvoort, where he qualified on the front row for the first time, led the race on lap one and set a new lap record while running second to Jochen

Rindt's radical new Lotus 72. Ickx had to stop on lap 51 to replace a punctured tire, losing a lap in the pits but still finishing a strong third. For this race Ickx had as his teammate Clay Regazzoni, whose debut was just as promising as Giunti's. Regazzoni qualified sixth and although his inexperience dropped him to ninth on the opening lap, he climbed steadily through the field to a fourth-place finish behind his team leader. Regazzoni's car had a different cockpit fairing, with a more abrupt windscreen than the original curved type used by Ickx.

It was now clear that the 312 B was as fast as anything in Formula 1, including the Lotus 72. Ickx emphasized this at Clermont-Ferrand, qualifying for

In front here, Ickx battled Rindt throughout the Hockenheim race, finished second to the Austrian.

the pole position and leading the French Grand Prix easily for fourteen laps. What seemed to the crowd to be a likely victory was lost through a burned valve which caused Ickx to retire; actually, his mechanics were aware of a cracked valve seat before the start and the retirement was expected, but not before putting up a show of the car's pace. It was Giunti's turn in the second Ferrari but he qualified only eleventh and ended up fourteenth, three laps behind, because of a power loss from over-revving early in the race.

Ickx and Regazzoni were respectively third and sixth fastest in practice at Brands Hatch, and the Swiss driver would certainly have been higher but for extensive brake problems during the sessions. The

recent indication of a basic lubrication problem on the 312 B—oil surge, especially on downhill curves—was countered by redesigned oil tanks with more elaborate baffling, used for the first time in the British race. Ickx had to take to the grass to stay ahead of Jack Brabham on the opening lap, although once ahead the 312 B built up a substantial lead. But for the second race in a row a demonstration of Ferrari superiority was cut short by mechanical failure, this time the differential giving up on the seventh lap. Regazzoni, however, drove consistently into fourth place.

Hockenheim, the present site of the German Grand Prix, was used as a championship Formula 1 circuit for the first time in 1970, a temporary expedient while improvements were made to the far more interesting but dangerous Nürburgring. A high-speed slipstreaming track in comparison to the classic winding circuit, Hockenheim saw a wheel-to-wheel battle between Ferrari and Lotus over the entire distance, Ickx leading for 31 of the 50 laps, Regazzoni for two of them and their rival Rindt the other 17. But Regazzoni spun off the track and Ickx found his straight-away speed insufficient to prevent the Lotus from slipstreaming past him at will; Rindt did this on the next to last lap and won by just 0.7 second. Nevertheless, with second place and the fastest lap, Ickx had has best result so far and a victory seemed imminent.

Boxer Dominant

IT CAME CONVINCINGLY at the Österreichring in the middle of August. For the first time there were three 312 Bs entered, for Ickx, Regazzoni and Giunti, and a fourth was available as a spare. Modifications to their Lucas fuel-injection metering units gave them significantly more mid-range torque, with peak power now 460 bhp at 11,600 rpm. Although Rindt managed to put his Lotus on the pole, just 0.46 second quicker than Regazzoni's time of 1:39.70, the three Ferraris sat one each on the first three rows, Ickx third fastest at 1:39.86 and Giunti behind him at 1:40.21. With the *ferragosto* holiday putting practically the whole nation out on the roads, a large contingent of Italians had journeyed to Austria to see the red cars win. They were not disappointed. Regazzoni made an excellent start and led the first lap from Ickx, who had also powered past Rindt, and Giunti was holding fourth behind the Lotus. Ickx went in front on lap two, leading Regazzoni for the next 58 laps to a runaway Ferrari one-two and the two drivers tied for fastest lap at 1:40.4. Giunti had to stop on lap 38 to replace a tire which had thrown some tread; he lost six places but worked his way back to finish seventh.

It had definitely been a 12-cylinder race, with BRMs taking fourth and fifth and Jean-Pierre Beltoise's Matra sixth after running third to the Ferraris for most of the race. The Ford Cosworth DFV-

25

powered cars seemed outclassed, the fastest of them, Rindt's Lotus, blowing up at 20 laps and only Rolf Stommelen's Brabham, which finished third, scoring points. After a slow start but with steady improvement throughout the season, Ferrari had taken command of Formula 1, a position the Italian team had not enjoyed for six years.

Another Ferrari victory at Monza, scored by Regazzoni after mastering a group of slipstreamers and moving away to a six-second margin at the flag, was overshadowed by the death of their main rival in practice. Rindt's loss was doubly tragic because he had already scored enough points to all but clinch the World Championship. Theoretically, five drivers had slim mathematical chances of surpassing his total, but only Ickx and Regazzoni had the cars capable of it. This Ferrari superiority had been demonstrated clearly in practice for the Italian race, with Ickx on the pole, Regazzoni behind him and Giunti again in row three. To gain extra top end on the high-speed track the 312 Bs were running a much flatter wing without the trailing edge. While Regazzoni's car ran perfectly throughout the race and also set the fastest lap, Ferrari reliability was not a strong point; Giunti's 312 B dropped out on lap 15 with an overheated fuel metering unit (he had been as high as fifth) and Ickx's transmission failed on lap 26 (he had led the race and seemed the most likely winner).

Ferrari took just two cars to North America for Ickx and Regazzoni and scored another one-two victory at St. Jovite after outlasting Stewart's promising new Tyrrell, which took pole position and led the first third of the race. By winning the Canadian race, Ickx kept his championship possibilities alive; moving to within 17 points of Rindt's posthumous total, he still had a good chance, even if he had to score the maximum possible 18 in the final two events.

Ickx put his 312 B on the pole at Watkins Glen but Lotus's new driver, the Brazilian Emerson Fittipaldi, saved the title for Rindt by winning the United States Grand Prix. Ickx had been running second to Stewart until the lap 57 when he stopped to repair a fractured fuel line, dropped to twelfth position, one lap behind, and lost all hope of winning the race. He struggled back to a fourth-place finish and Regazzoni, making two stops for tire and ignition problems, finished a lowly thirteenth, seven laps behind. Although Ferrari enthusiasts were disappointed by this result, there were many relieved to have the late Rindt confirmed as World Champion.

But Ferrari was the power in Formula 1 now, rubbing it in with yet another Ickx-Regazzoni one-two in Mexico. Again Stewart's Tyrrell was their main challenger, but Ferrari was in command of the situation, leading the whole distance and carrying away all the honors: Regazzoni had qualified on the pole

and Ickx drove the fastest race lap.

Scuderia Ferrari had come from nowhere in 1969 to almost complete domination in the second half of 1970. The final statistics read: Four victories (three of them one-twos), five pole positions and seven fastest laps. The 312 B earned Ferrari second place in the Manufacturer's Championship (with 52 scorable points, a vast improvement over the seven earned in 1969!) and took its three pilots to second, third and seventeenth positions in the Drivers' Championship (Ickx with 40 points, Regazzoni 33 and Giunti 3). Regazzoni's score was all the more remarkable for his only having run in eight of the 13 races; the Swiss driver had been noted for his wildness as a Formula 2 driver but had shown both maturity and speed against the world's best in Formula 1. Ickx, after only three full seasons in Grand Prix racing, was at the height of his career.

Making Way for the B2

A NEW DESIGN known as the 312 B2 (Chapter 4) was already under development for 1971 but the four existing 312 Bs were employed for the opening races of the season. Ickx and Regazzoni stayed on as the main drivers; Ignazio Giunti died in a freak accident at Buenos Aires when leading the 1000-km race in the new boxer-engined 312 PB sports car (Chapter 9)

Forghieri's expression does not suggest the overwhelming victory Ferrari would achieve in Austria. After Ickx-Regazzoni 1-2, drivers had to hide from fans in transporter at left.

Ferrari's 1970 Formula 1 team: Gianclaudio Regazzoni, Ignazio Giunti and Jacky Ickx, before the Italian Grand Prix at Monza.

Regazzoni's victory at Monza drove Italian fans even wilder than in Austria. He can be seen at center of mob just below right column.

Poor Ferrari performance at Watkins Glen ended Ickx' chances to beat Rindt's posthumus total.

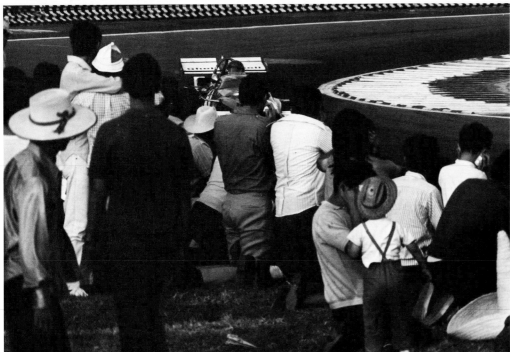

Mexican spectators seem more concerned about their ears than vulnerability of their bodies; Ickx, just visible, led another Ferrari 1-2.

Andretti, leading Donohue's F 5000 here, won second consecutive race for Ferrari at Ontario.

Italian-born American Mario Andretti joined Ferrari in 1971, won debut race at Kyalami.

Last major race for 312 B was 1971 Spanish GP; Ickx, ultimately second, leads Regazzoni at start.

With 312 B2 running most 1971 races, 312 Bs were used mainly for practice; this is Regazzoni in the older car on the Nurburgring.

and his place on the Formula 1 team was taken by Mario Andretti. At that time the American USAC star, winner of the 1969 Indianapolis race, had limited Grand Prix experience (a few races for Lotus in 1968-69 and an unrewarding season driving a March in 1970) but his road-racing ability was already apparent.

It was Andretti who continued the 312 B's run of successes by winning the championship-opener at Kyalami at the beginning of March and the non-championship event at Ontario Motor Speedway in California at the end of the month. A single 312 B2 was present at Kyalami (crashed by Regazzoni in practice) while the 312 Bs, basically unchanged from 1970 except for the lower-profile Firestone tires, were the race entries. Regazzoni was the fastest of the three Ferraris in qualifying, starting from the front row, with Andretti in the second rank; Ickx was uncharacteristically slow, starting eighth. All three cars were troubled by vibrations from the new-type Firestones and the team did not start the race with the greatest confidence. Nevertheless, Regazzoni led the first 16 laps, until passed by Denis Hulme's new McLaren M19; Clay gradually lost ground but Andretti just as steadily moved up behind Hulme in second place. The American dramatically increased his pace as he closed on Hulme, setting the fastest time just before taking the lead four laps from the end. As Hulme had dropped back with suspension trouble, Regazzoni came in a satisfactory third behind Stewart, but Ickx, delayed a lap replacing a flat tire, completed a discouraging weekend in eighth position. Andretti described his Ferrari victory as "the happiest day of my life," surprising in comparison to his far more lucrative Indianapolis win but perhaps a more emotional milestone in view of his Italian boyhood.

Only two 312 Bs went to Ontario for Ickx and

Ickx' 312 B was faster than his B2 at Watkins Glen, gave him the fastest lap in the race.

Andretti, Regazzoni having given the 312 B2 a victorious debut in the non-championship race at Brands Hatch, England, the week before. Ickx was no more fortunate in the two-heat Questor event than he had been at Kyalami, being slowed in the first part by a puncture and colliding with Josef Siffert's BRM in the second. Andretti had destroyed the front end of his 312 B in practice but took the repaired car to convincing wins ahead of Stewart in both heats, and the overall aggregate.

The last major race for the 312 B chassis was the Spanish Grand Prix, run at Barcelona in 1971. Chassis 003, 004 and 002 were qualified respectively first, second and eighth by Ickx, Regazzoni and Andretti. A single 312 B2 practiced, only briefly, Regazzoni being about four seconds slower than with his regular car. Ickx led the first five laps before giving way to Stewart, running a processional second until near the finish, when he reduced the Scot's advantage from eight seconds to 3.4 and lowered the lap record in the process. But the Tyrrell had broken Ferrari's string of successes, and even more distressing were the retirements of Regazzoni (an engine misfire and finally a fire in the pits resulting from a broken fuel pump mounting) and Andretti (two fuel pump failures, causing fires both times).

The 312 B chassis were used in practice at Monte Carlo, Zandvoort, Nürburgring, Monza, Mosport and Watkins Glen, but actually raced in only four more events. The non-championship Jochen Rindt Memorial Trophy race at Hockenheim saw the final victory of the 312 B; appropriately, Ickx qualified first, set the fastest lap and won easily. Regazzoni had qualified second and followed Ickx closely at first but lost ten laps with a short in the rev-limiter circuit, ending up fourteenth and last. This spoiled team manager Peter Schetty's plan to have his two drivers cruise along in one-two formation until given the free-for-all signal five laps from the end. With prize money but no championship points at stake, this was no great risk for Ferrari and would have made an interesting finish.

Andretti drove a 312 B at Zandvoort, qualifying way down in 18th position and retiring on lap four with another fuel pump failure. Ickx returned to the older chassis at Monza, qualifying second (on Goodyear tires, although Firestones were used in the race) but dropping out after 15 laps with a failure of the Pirelli crankshaft damper. At Mosport in Canada, Regazzoni's 312 B was easily the fastest of all the Ferraris in practice, but an engine failure forced him to switch to the 312 B2 for the race.

The final outing for the 312 B was at Watkins Glen, Ickx finding the spare chassis faster than his regular 312 B2. Although he retired from the race with a broken alternator on lap 49, he had been running a strong second to Francois Cevert's Tyrrell and had set the fastest lap on lap 43. Not bad for Ferrari's *old* chassis.

Better Than its Successor

THE 1971 RECORD of the 312 B was three wins, two pole positions and four fastest laps from seven races, a better record than that of its successor, the 312 B2. As the discussion of the 312 B2's career in Chapter 4 makes apparent, the abandonment of the original 312 B was almost certainly premature. Its detail improvement might have been more rewarding than the immediate development of the 312 B2, with its many new and not entirely successful features. As it was, Ferrari dominated two half seasons with the 312 B but did not gain the World Championship. Nevertheless, the first-generation 3-liter boxer had won seven Grand Prix races and re-established the supremacy of Maranello technology.

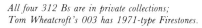

All four 312 Bs are in private collections;
Tom Wheatcroft's 003 has 1971-type Firestones.

Chapter 4

312 B2 F1 **Advantage Lost**

THE SUCCESSFUL DEBUT of the 312 B2, by Clay Regazzoni at Brands Hatch in March 1971, was misleading. In fact, the beginning of the season, in which Ferrari won five of the first seven races and came second and third in the other two, was misleading. Ferrari dominance, built up so systematically throughout 1970, was short-lived. After his victory in the Dutch Grand Prix in June, Jacky Ickx was a close second to Jackie Stewart in the World Championship standings, but the Ferrari team leader did not score a single point during the remainder of 1971. There were three basic reasons for the nosedive in Ferrari fortunes: the performance of the rival Tyrrell chassis, the emergence of a serious lubrication problem on the 312 B engine, and the failure of the B2 chassis, particularly the novel rear suspension, to realize its potential.

The 312 B2 was unveiled for the press, inside the main assembly plant at Maranello, in mid-winter, and the initial testing took place on the Modena circuit in February. In appearance, the B2 looked like a widened and flattened 312 B. The central chassis/ body structure, more angular than its predecessor and with a wedge-shaped profile, was still of aluminum-skinned tubular design rather than a true monocoque. Only at the very back did the B2 depart from the basic configuration of the 312 B. A complex rear suspension had been designed, utilizing nearly-horizontal inboard coil springs and shock absorbers operated by triangulated upper members attached to the top of the wheel uprights. Single, upper, radius rods were used (Ferrari was to vacillate over the merits of single and double radius rods for more than five years!) while simple A-arms located the uprights at the bottom. With inboard brakes, a circuitous anti-roll bar linkage and the mounting of the engine oil radiators just in front of the springs, this was a complicated rear end, with an airflow in which the rear wing could hardly be efficient. The theoretical advantages of this geometry, mainly keeping a large area of the rear tires in contact with the road, were more than offset by the practical disadvantages, including too much play in whole system and a greater sensitivity to tire vibration. (The 15-inch treadless rear Firestones created problems in this respect, and Ferrari suffered more than most.) Cynical observers said Forghieri couldn't leave well enough alone, and unfortunately they were right.

Although he could not run in all the events because of USAC commitments, Mario Andretti joined Ickx and Regazzoni on the Formula 1 team (Giunti was killed in a sports car race in Buenos Aires). Three of the 312 B chassis were taken to South Africa at the beginning of March, plus a lone 312 B2 which Regazzoni gave a test run at Kyalami. The handling of the latter was unpredictable at best, and Regazzoni spun and badly damaged it in practice. But this ominous beginning was seemingly overcome only two weeks later when Regazzoni won the Daily Mail Race of Champions at Brands Hatch (despite its name, not counting toward the championship). The win was the result of a fortunate choice of the right tires for the event, which started out wet but ended on a nearly dry track. Nevertheless, Clay had driven a good race, the rear suspension of the B2 had benefited from a reduction in much of the flexing noted in South Africa, and Ferrari was encouraged.

Just one B2 was taken to the next championship race, at Barcelona, and Regazzoni was 3.4 seconds slower with it in practice than with the 312 B he used in the race. The first championship event in which the B2s were entered as race machines was Monte Carlo; the cars now had a more streamlined headrest

Regazzoni tests 312 B2 at Modena, February 1971.

fairing and wing mount, and revised oil-cooler ducting, with NACA scoops in the top of the rear bodywork extension. Ickx qualified for the front row next to Stewart and finished 3rd, behind the Scot and Ronnie Peterson. Regazzoni qualified only 11th fastest, more than two seconds slower than Ickx; in the race he hit a barrier, made a pit stop to replace the two damaged wheels, but retired with suspension troubles after 24 laps. Stewart had also won at Barcelona; while the pattern was not yet completely

Press debut of 312 B2 was at Maranello,
where Fiat Dinos were coming off assembly line.
Rear suspension had novel inboard springs.

Race debut of 312 B2 resulted in deceptive victory for Regazzoni at Brands Hatch.

Best 1971 race for 312 B2 was Ickx' hard-fought win over Rodriguez' BRM at Zandvoort.

*Ickx qualified second and finished third in
his first race with B2 at Monte Carlo.*

*Regazzoni spun and crushed nose of his 312 B2
but hung on to finish third in Dutch Grand Prix.*

clear, he was well on the way to a second World Championship.

A Win in Holland

BUT FERRARI WAS TO ENJOY one more success in 1971, a strong performance by Ickx in the rainy Dutch Grand Prix at Zandvoort. The Belgian qualified on the pole, overcame a relentless challenge by Pedro Rodriguez in the BRM and won by eight seconds, setting the fastest lap to boot. Regazzoni qualified fourth and ran a steady, supportive third throughout the race, but even he was lapped by the leading pair. Andretti had qualified his B2 eighth fastest in the first practice session but crashed it when one of the 17-inch rear tires came off the rim; as the same thing had happened to Regazzoni, Forghieri put all the cars back on regular 15-inch rims for the race. In Andretti's case, the B2 was not repairable in time, so he started 18th in the back-up 312 B and retired with fuel pump failure after three

laps. In addition to trying the 17-inch Firestones, the B2s had different Koni shock absorbers to improve the handling.

After the result at Zandvoort, Ferrari came to the Paul Ricard circuit in France with some confidence, the only changes being the safety rims to keep the tires from coming off the wheels. But despite the 470 bhp now being produced at 12,500 rpm by the flat-12 engine, Ferrari was surprised by the superior straight-line speed of Stewart's Tyrrell, which was consistently a second faster than Regazzoni or Ickx throughout the practice sessions. The Ferrari drivers qualified second and third on the front row, but Stewart simply drove away from them in the race. Ickx had a crankshaft break after four laps, the first of a series of lubrication-related failures that plagued the 312 B engine in 1971, while Regazzoni hung on to second place for 20 laps, losing nearly a second a lap to Stewart, before spinning off on oil dropped by Peterson's engine. This was the first time in nearly a year that Ferrari had failed to score championship

312 B2s get off the line a little better than Stewart's Tyrrell at Paul Ricard but he ran away from them before the Ferraris retired.

points. Worse was to come.

For the British Grand Prix at Silverstone the 312 B2s had semi-streamlined front wheel fairings fitted to the ends of the front wings; these were limited by the rules to a width equal to the front track. Regazzoni was especially fast at Silverstone, setting the pole time that was later equaled by Stewart. He led the Scot for three laps (Ickx, who had qualified sixth, moved up on the first lap to give Ferrari a temporary 1-2) and settled into second place, which he held for two-thirds of the race. But the engine lost its oil pressure and Regazzoni had to retire after a stop to replace a front tire on lap 48. Ickx had also had the same tire problem and his engine gave up on lap 52.

Ferrari was in serious trouble. Partly because of the vibration problems with the Firestone tires, and mainly because of the unwieldy rear suspension layout, no progress was being made in chassis handling; now, lubrication trouble was destroying the previously taken-for-granted engine reliability. Andretti drove a third B2 at the Nürburgring, joining Ickx and Regazzoni; this was only the second time the American had been to the difficult German circuit, his previous outing having been less than one race lap in 1969 with the four-wheel-drive Lotus 63. The Ferrari team had not been to the Nürburgring since 1968 (the team skipped the 1969 race and Hockenheim was used for the German Grand Prix in 1970) but had long experience there previously. Ickx was also a master on the winding circuit and was able to put his B2 on the front row, second to—guess who?—Jackie Stewart. Regazzoni, without Formula 1 experience at the Ring, went very fast; he had a spectacular crash in practice but went even faster after his car was rebuilt to qualify fourth. Andretti was more than 12 seconds slower than Ickx and started eleventh. Ickx led Stewart briefly on the first lap but dropped behind and then went off the track on lap 2. Regazzoni was third all the way and Andretti learned the way around fast enough to finish a very satisfactory fourth. But Stewart had won his third race in a row, and Ferrari was no

Ferrari tried fairings for front tires and engine intakes in July test at Modena; former were used at Silverstone only and latter were abandoned.

Regazzoni started from the pole at Silverstone but his and Ickx' engines both failed.

longer challenging.

Both Ickx and Regazzoni retired from the Austrian Grand Prix, the scene of the 312 B's first triumph a year before. The Belgian's car ran far back on about eight cylinders before stopping altogether with faulty spark plug leads; Regazzoni had battled for third place but his engine failed.

Putting up a show for the Italian crowd he had thrilled the year before, Regazzoni led the first three laps of the Italian Grand Prix; Ickx was also among the leading group of slipstreamers, but both Ferraris dropped out with a failure of the vibration damper mounted at the end of the crankshaft. Aerodynamically the cars were faster in a straight line, with wide-chord, single-plane rear wings; Monza requires less downforce, having no low-speed corners. This was just as well, as Ferrari had not yet learned (nor had many teams) how important it was to get clean air *under* the rear airfoil, and this was almost completely blocked off by the oil cooler ducts.

Ferrari was simply uncompetitive at Mosport. Any positive development of the B2 had come to a standstill and Regazzoni was fastest of the Ferraris with the old 312 B, but its engine broke and he had to use a B2, which set him back to eighteenth on the grid and spun off the damp track in the race. Ickx and Andretti were hardly better, with twelfth and twenty-third starting positions respectively; in the race they came in eighth and thirteenth.

The final race of 1971 was at Watkins Glen. This time Ickx used the 312 B, finding it more than a second faster than his regular B2. Regazzoni went well enough to start from the second row, while Andretti would have started from the third, with Ickx, if a postponed USAC race had not required his appearance. Ickx ran the 312 B, getting as high as second and setting the fastest lap as discussed in Chapter 3, while Regazzoni's brought him home sixth.

What had happened in 1971? In addition to the suspension, tire and engine problems already mentioned, it is apparent that Ferrari slipped into one of the periods of depression, almost melancholy, which occasionally haunts the team when technical solutions are not immediately forthcoming. If the last half of 1970 and the first half of 1971 had made a single season, Ferrari would have cleaned up everything in sight. But Ferrari was not the only team to be decimated by Stewart's superiority.

In its first season, the 312 B2 was far from a total failure, having scored two victories and having led four other races, however briefly. But it sorely lacked development potential, and 1972 was going to be just as difficult as 1971.

Rethinking the B2

ATTACKING THE TWO PROBLEMS that had plagued the team most, poor engine lubrication and indifferent handling, Ferrari tested a revised 312 B2 at Modena in October, driven by Regazzoni and Peter Schetty.

For the former problem, as a temporary measure while internal engine changes were being studied, two supplementary oil tanks were mounted, one on each side of the body ahead of the engine. The rear suspension was entirely redesigned to deal with the handling deficiency; the novel inboard coil-spring arrangement was abandoned in favor of a more conventional system, with upper and lower radius arms, single upper links, reversed lower A-arms and outboard coil spring/shock units. This layout proved much more effective, especially with the 13-inch Firestone rear tires now being used.

Regazzoni did this to his 312 B2 in Nurburgring practice but finished third in the race.

The three 312 B2 chassis taken to Buenos Aires in January 1972 for Ickx, Regazzoni and Andretti had the revised rear suspension but the new bottom-end design had apparently solved the engine lubrication problems, and no external tankage was required. As is often necessary in the Southern-hemisphere summer races, a larger radiator opening gave better cooling in the hot weather. Regazzoni, Ickx and Andretti qualified sixth, eighth, and ninth, no real improvement in form, but the cars were more raceworthy, reliability bringing Ickx and Regazzoni into third and fourth positions after steady drives. Andretti, troubled by persistent misfiring, retired on lap 21 after several stops.

At Kyalami the B2s appeared with ''Tyrrell'' or ''sports car'' type full-width noses, which had been tested at Modena by Schetty the week before. Regazzoni qualified for the front row, three-tenths of a second slower than Stewart, but made a bad start and was way down in twelfth place at the end of the first lap. He worked his way up as high as seventh but pitted on lap 52 to replace a punctured tire and ended up twelfth. Andretti, winner here in 1971, was again the most successful Ferrari driver, finishing fourth, while Ickx, whose start was as poor as Regazzoni's, came in eighth with an engine clearly lacking power. But the South African event had at least seen

Ickx led at the start but crashed on the first lap.

Andretti's best race in a B2 was his fourth place in the 1971 German Grand Prix.

*Wide-chord rear wings were used at Monza;
Regazzoni could not repeat 1970 triumph.*

*Supplementary oil tanks were tested in October
1971 to cure lubrication failures, along with
new rear suspension with conventional springs.*

*Ickx was third at Buenos Aires in first 1972
race; note chopped nose and stacked rear wings.*

Schetty tests Tyrrell-type nose in April 1972.

41

Mechanics fit rain tires to 312 B2s during practice at Jarama; dry tires were used in the race. Ickx started from the pole and set the fastest lap but finished second to Fittipaldi.

all three Ferraris finish, for the first time in almost a year.

While the "sport car" noses were tried in practice, the standard pieces were used again at Jarama, where Ickx restored Ferrari prestige by qualifying on the pole, nearly a second faster than the next group of cars, setting the fastest lap in the race and finishing second behind Emerson Fittipaldi's Lotus 72. Regazzoni finished third, a lap behind his team leader, while Andretti dropped out with a piston failure just two laps after he had passed Hulme's Mclaren into fourth place; at that point all three Ferraris were running in the first six, an encouraging performance.

Andretti was not entered at Monte Carlo, which came on the same weekend as the first Indianapolis qualifying session. Ickx and Regazzoni emphasized Ferrari's restored competitiveness by qualifying second and third fastest behind Fittipaldi, but it was Jean-Pierre Beltoise in a BRM who won a torrential race by seizing the lead and throwing spray at his pursuers for the 80 laps. Ickx was his closest pursuer for the whole race, coming home second, but Regazzoni had an accident on lap 52 trying to hold third place against the pressure of Stewart's Tyrrell.

The Belgian Grand Prix, not run in 1971 and held at Spa-Francorchamps in the years before that, came to a new circuit, Nivelles, for the 1972 event in June. Although starting from respectable (second and fourth) grid positions, the Ferraris did not have a good race. Ickx and Regazzoni were part of an intense five-way battle for second place but both dropped out, the Belgian driver with throttle-linkage trouble and the Swiss after colliding with the spinning Tecno of Nanni Galli.

Galli's encounter with Regazzoni in Belgium did not prevent the Italian from taking a temporary spot on the Ferrari team in the next race at Clermont-Ferrand in France, replacing Regazzoni (who had a broken wrist, not sustained at Nivelles but in an amateur soccer match) in the third 312 B2. But Galli did not make anything of his opportunity, qualifying in nineteenth position, over seven seconds slower than Amon's Matra and five seconds worse than Ickx's fourth-place time. In the race both Ferraris were lapped, but Ickx had run a strong second to Stewart before stopping with a puncture. This put him down in a disappointing eleventh place; Galli was thirteenth, having run near the back of the field the whole time. A further revised rear suspension was used in France, dispensing with the lower radius arms.

As Regazzoni was still *hors de combat* two weeks later, the second Ferrari seat at Brands Hatch was now offered to Arturo Merzario, an Italian with no previous Grand Prix experience but a decided flair, already demonstrated in the 312 PB sports/racing car. Ickx qualified on the pole and led for two-thirds of the British race before he was sidelined by a leaking oil radiator, so it was the rookie who salvaged

some Ferrari honor by bringing his 312 B2 into sixth place, an excellent debut. The rear wings were mounted much further back at Brands Hatch, to get them away from the complicated brake and oil-radiator ducting, but were still operating in turbulent air and not really effective.

The B2's Best Race

THE PERFORMANCE EARNED Merzario another drive in the next race at the Nürburgring; Regazzoni was back in action but Andretti was still occupied in USAC races on the other side of the Atlantic. The German race was easily Ferrari's greatest Formula 1 accomplishment of 1972, and a convincing demonstration on the world's most demanding race course. Ickx, always a Ring master since his astounding Formula 2 drive in the 1967 race, started from the pole and led every lap, averaging 116.63 mph, faster than the previous lap record, and setting a new record of 117.81 mph on lap 10. Regazzoni never ran lower than fourth and came in a solid second, 48 seconds behind Ickx. Merzario did not approach the speed of his teammates but his car had been damaged in a crash during practice and the suspension was clearly not right; he did finish (twelfth) and give Ferrari 100-percent reliability to go with the 1-2 victory.

Three cars turned up at the Österreichring but only Ickx and Regazzoni were entered. The success in Germany was not to be repeated in Austria, both cars retiring without fuel pressure. Regazzoni had at least started from the front row, running second to Stewart for the first three laps, but Ickx was never in contention. To improve rear-wing airflow, the headrest fairings were abbreviated, almost resembling the shape that was to be used years later on the 312 T2 and T3.

For Monza the wings were mounted still further to the rear, with single wide-chord airfoils replacing the previous two-foil stacked configuration. Combined with the boxer engine's power, these chassis gave competitive results. Ickx started on the pole, Regazzoni was fourth fastest and Andretti, back in Formula 1, was seventh. But Ferrari's hopes of an Italian victory, raised by Ickx leading most of the race and Regazzoni running with him in first or second place, were not realized. Regazzoni was involved in a crash with Carlos Pace's March on lap 17 and Ickx's car had an electrical failure just ten laps from the end, when he was running ahead of the Lotus 72 of the new World Champion, Fittipaldi. Ickx had the consolation of another fastest lap, while Andretti was the sole finisher for Maranello, coming in seventh. Mario had been fourth on the first lap, so all three Ferraris showed speed.

Three chassis, in essentially the same form as raced at Monza, went to North America for the Canadian and U.S. Grands Prix. Regazzoni and Ickx drove at Mosport, neither showing pace in practice or the race, their finishing positions being fifth

Detail of mid-1972 rear wing and oil cooler
arrangement, as seen on B2 at Clermont-Ferrand.

Ickx puts a wheel on the curb in the T-car at
Brands Hatch; he gained the pole with number 5.

Nanni Galli replaced an injured Regazzoni in
France; leading Reutemann here, he was thirteenth.

Merzario, Regazzoni's stand-in at Brands, did
better than Galli, finished a good sixth.

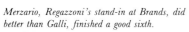

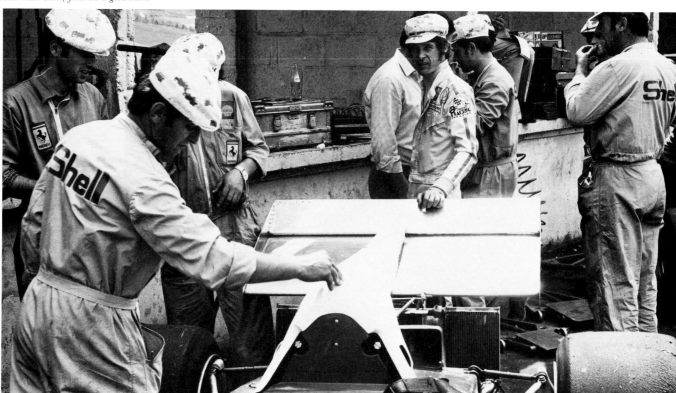

Ickx, a Nurburgring master, won the 312 B2's finest victory in 1972; here, oversteering slightly, he lifts a rear wheel as he exits the Karussel. Regazzoni made it a Ferrari 1-2.

Garage shot of Ickx's car shows semi-monocoque.

Rear-positioned single airfoil wing at Monza worked better but brake scoops and oil coolers still compromised its efficiency.

Regazzoni started second at the Osterreichring but succumbed to failing fuel pressure. Note the shortened headrest to give better wing flow.

Mechanics wet down Regazzoni's tires at
Monza before a qualifying attempt.

Last race for 312 B2 was 1973 Kyalami; Ickx
retired and Merzario, shown, came in fourth.

*Giulio Borsari, one of Ferrari's longest serving
and most able mechanics, at Monza in 1972.*

and twelfth respectively. Andretti joined them for his
own national Grand Prix at Watkins Glen. Again,
speed was lacking (although Ickx got as high as
fourth) and the three Ferrari pilots finished fifth,
sixth and eighth in the order Ickx, Andretti, Regazzoni. Development had clearly not continued after
the disappointment at Monza; a new design team
was at work on the 312 B3 for 1973 and the B2 was
at the end of its career.

Although results were not outstanding, the 312 B2
had a decent year in 1972, especially considering the
formidable opposition of Fittipaldi/Lotus and Stewart/
Tyrrell. The B2 was usually competitive, its four
pole positions and three fastest laps making it the
pacesetter on those occasions, while the 1-2 triumph
in Germany was a one-race performance not bettered
by any team. The handling had become more than
manageable (the Nürburgring walkaway proved
that!) and the engine failures of 1971 were countered
by the redesign.

The B2 chassis had three more races to run,
however; the B3 development was still not complete
as the 1973 season opened. Regazzoni and Andretti

left the team, the former to drive for BRM and the
latter the new Parnelli, although his Formula 1
commitment was still secondary to USAC. Ferrari
signed just one driver to back up Ickx: Merzario,
who had done so well in his debut at Brands Hatch.
The pair raced in South America and in South
Africa with 312 B2s that showed no further development but were moderately effective considering their
age. Ickx qualified third for both Buenos Aires and
Interlagos, finishing fourth and fifth respectively.
Merzario, much slower in practice, had ninth and
fourth place finishes, passing his team leader in
Brazil when Ickx had a pit stop to replace a tire
damaged by broken glass on the track; he had been
running a good third at the time.

In their last race, at Kyalami, the 312 B2s were
dead slow, starting from lowly eleventh and fifteenth
grid positions. Ickx was out after an accident on lap
2 but Merzario showed the B2's reliability by driving
it steadily through the field to fourth place. Two
years before, the replacement of the 312 B had been
premature; now the retirement of the 312 B2 was
clearly overdue.

47

Chapter 5

312 B3 F1 **Difficult Development**

THE FERRARI 312 B3 was really three different cars, one an apparent total failure that was never raced, the second an ineffective machine that gave the team its most discouraging season since 1969, and the third a vastly improved, race-winning car that brought Maranello back to near-championship form. It seemed that Ferrari persisted with the B3 designation until they had a car that could give it an honorable place in the record books. In this they were ultimately successful.

The first 312 B3 has been and will probably always remain something of a mystery car. Designed by Ing. Forghieri and carrying chassis number 009, it was tested during the summer of 1972, possibly with a Monza debut in mind. When revealed to the press in August, it immediately received the nickname *Spazzaneve* (Snowplow). The name was certainly appropriate, as the photos clearly show. But the car did not run at Monza and never competed in any race.

Its extremely wide, flat, semi-monocoque structure had twin side radiators, mounted behind the front suspension, and the downswept, shovel-like nose had two large NACA-shaped intakes ducted to them. The rear suspension was like that of the early 1972 312 B2, with double radius rods, while in front the upper arms had additional tubular radius rods angled to the rear. Photos of the car have shown minor variations in engine air intakes; it was tested with recessed, NACA-shaped ducts and with scoops raised

Wide, flat-topped 1972 312 B3 was never raced. Shovel-like nose had intakes for side-mounted radiators, earned nickname Spazzaneve *(Snowplow).*

above the body. In the latter case, it is likely that different fuel-injection trumpet lengths were also under study. The rear wing was set well forward, at a huge angle of incidence, instead of toward the rear as on the Monza B2s; this suggests that the development of the *Spazzaneve* had already been abandoned earlier in the year. Whatever its other shortcomings, it must have had very poor aerodynamics, with great frontal area, disturbed air flow and sharply-angled rear wing. This is easy to say in the light of further aerodynamic progress; the *Spazzaneve* certainly looked exciting in 1972.

No firm technical data has been released by the factory (it is hard enough getting historical information on Ferrari's successes!) but the *Spazzaneve* had a wheelbase of approximately 2300 mm and a weight of 540 kg. It was eventually sold to Pierre Bardinon and at the time of writing it resided in the collection of Englishman Anthony Bamford. Perhaps to vindicate himself, Mauro Forghieri has since described the *Spazzaneve* as "a running laboratory to verify new solutions, an experiment that was invaluable in projecting later versions. Even the 312 T utilized the lessons of the first unique prototype."

A completely different 312 B3, credited to engineers Forghieri, Franco Rocchi and Giancarlo Bussi, made its appearance in February 1973. Its development was entrusted to engineers Sandro Colombo, who came to Ferrari from Fiat, and Giorgio Ferrari (no relation to Enzo); it seemed that Forghieri was in the "doghouse" a result of the *Spazzaneve* project. In retrospect, it is clear that the 1973 B3 was an interim car and that Colombo took charge of its development while Forghieri studied more advanced concepts that would give greater long-term rewards.

The 312 B3 shown to the press in February was the first Ferrari Formula 1 car with a true monocoque chassis; to save time the first tubs were built in England by John Thompson. Initially, the car had side-mounted water radiators, set just ahead of the engine with large NACA ducts in the sides of the body. There were some visual similarities to the *Spazzaneve*, such as the flat chassis and the raised engine scoops, but the nose was flatter and free of any ducting, and the rear wing was set far back as

49

Jacky Ickx speculates on potential of his 1973 312 B3, first built with side radiators. Rear wing was set well back, above large oil tank.

312 B3 was raced with single nose radiator. Ickx discusses performance with Ing. Sandro Colombo in pits at Barcelona; he started twelfth.

on the late-1972 B2. The wheelbase was the longest yet at 2500 mm and the weight was 578 kg because of the deformable structure and other safety requirements of the 1973 regulations. The increased weight was countered by an engine output of 485 bhp at 12,500 rpm, just slightly above the 480 bhp of the 1972 312 B2. Ferrari switched to Goodyear tires as the Firestone program was no longer competitive, but the suspension design of the B3 differed from the B2 only in the omission of the lower rear radius rods (Ferrari vacillated between two and four rods no less than five times during the development of the 312 B, B2 and B3).

By the time of the B3's race debut at Barcelona at the end of April, it had already undergone a major change. The car raced by Ickx (Merzario was not entered) had a front-mounted radiator, while his back-up machine was of the original side-radiator configuration. The front-radiator version was the more effective and it was in this form that the 312 B3 was run until its major redesign by Forghieri in midseason. Ickx qualified it sixth fastest at Barcelona and ended up twelfth after brake trouble and a pit stop.

Again, only Ickx was entered for the Belgian race, both cars now being in front-radiator form (the side-mounted arrangement resulted in persistent overheating). At Zolder Ickx was able to qualify third and run in this position until he had an engine blow-up on lap 6 caused by an oil pump failure.

Merzario joined Ickx at Monte Carlo. Their 312 B3s were basically the same as the two seen at Zolder, except for the splitting of the radiator outlet

to allow for a small NACA intake in the center for cockpit cooling. Ickx could only qualify seventh and Merzario sixteenth, so Ferrari was clearly uncompetitive; in the race both retired, Ickx on lap 45 with a driveshaft failure and Merzario on lap 59 with a loss of oil pressure.

Ickx went solo again at Andertorp in Sweden, where he qualified only eighth quickest. He ran a lonely race in seventh position, challenging no one but moving up to sixth with the retirement of Fittipaldi on lap 76. Ferrari was in the doldrums; there was no apparent chassis development and, even worse, the team was losing the faith of its number one driver, a star performer for them when the cars were competitive.

The situation was obvious at Paul Ricard, where Ickx was down in twelfth starting spot and even Merzario was faster, though only tenth himself. At least Ferrari's usual reliability was present, both cars making it to the finish line. Ickx made a good start, coming around eighth on the first lap and moving up to fifth at the end as other cars dropped out. Merzario made a poor start, losing six places on the first lap, but also benefited from the attrition, coming in an eventual seventh.

Ickx was a miserable nineteenth in practice at Silverstone, and his ultimate eighth-place finish did nothing to restore the 312 B3's now hopeless reputation. What was wrong? There were three basic factors: a chassis design that was dated, heavy, and lacking in development potential; a development team that lacked sufficient ability to solve problems at the circuit; and a driver who no longer wished to commit his considerable ability to an unrewarding project.

Yet Another B3

FERRARI REGROUPED, giving the next two events at Zandvoort and the Nürburgring a miss (releasing Ickx temporarily to drive for McLaren in the German race) and completely rethinking the design of the B3. Whether he had been in the "doghouse" or an "ivory tower," Ing. Forghieri showed that his time away from the front lines had been well spent, returning to prominence with a drastically revised version of the Thompson-monocoque, Colombo-managed chassis. That this third-generation 312 B3 would be an instant world-beater was unrealistic, but its performance was so markedly improved that the future prospects were extremely bright.

While the monocoque was similar and the suspension layout the same, the new B3's components were relocated in the interests of improved weight distribution and aerodynamics. There were once again two side-mounted radiators, but these were placed obliquely (from the horizontal) just behind the front suspension, with outlets in the top of the bodywork. A large oil radiator was positioned at the left rear of the body, mounted longitudinally

Ickx leads Denis Hulme and Wilson Fittipaldi
at Monte Carlo, before breaking a driveshaft.

Close-ups at Paul Ricard show front and back
ends of Ickx' B3. Subframe held radiator; rear
radius rods traveled within air scoop housings.

Extensively modified 312 B3 S, with water radiators behind front suspension and oil radiator and tank
beside engine, appeared in Austria for Merzario.
Front and rear wings were much more effective.
Ickx' last Formula 1 drive for Ferrari was
in the revised 312 B3 S at Monza in 1973.

Merzario drove with this temporary nose after damaging front in practice for Canadian GP.

and fed by an angled scoop. Engine air was now taken in by a single scoop above the rollbar (this arrangement had already been tried on the boxer-engined 312 PB sports/racing car at the Nürburgring in May). And Forghieri had come up with basic front and rear wing concepts that would prove effective for all the Formula 1 boxers since, albeit with major detail refinements: a single full-width front plane mounted above the nose and a broad-chord rear plane mounted on a single central pylon.

Ickx did not return to the team for the Austrian Grand Prix, but Merzario showed the revised B3 (sometimes referred as 312 B3 S, although the two chassis so described were modified from the prev-

iously-constructed cars numbers 010 and 011) to be dramatically improved. The still relatively inexperienced Italian driver was able to qualify sixth fastest and run a strong fourth for three laps of the race. But it was an off-song boxer engine that reduced the car's debut performance, causing Merzario to slip back to a seventh-place finish.

The B3 S was not as competitive at Monza, Merzario qualifying seventh and Ickx, back with Ferrari for what was to be their last race together, still showing his disillusionment by qualifying fourteenth. In fairness, Ickx's performance in practice was hampered by an engine failure, and he was complimentary of the car's redesign, saying it was lighter to steer and more balanced in all attitudes. In the race he drove unremarkably to eighth place while Merzario, eager to do well on his home circuit, overdid things and hit the curbing of the chicane on the second lap, damaging his suspension too much to continue.

Only one car was sent to North America for Merzario to drive in the Canadian and U.S. Grands Prix. The effort was minimal, it being clear that Ferrari considered the results of these two events less important than the further redesign of the B3 for the 1974 season. And as Merzario was not one of the drivers signed for the following year, neither his nor the car's performances at Mosport and Watkins Glen can be considered significant. His finishes were respectively fifteenth and sixteenth. The star performer, though not the winner, at Mosport was Niki Lauda, the Austrian driver who was Clay Regazzoni's BRM teammate in 1973.

Major change to B3 for 1974 was forward position of cockpit; Regazzoni returned to Ferrari team with third place, fastest lap at Buenos Aires, second at Interlagos.

Regazzoni, Lauda and Montezemolo

THE RETURN OF REGAZZONI to the Ferrari team for 1974 was of great significance, for with him came Lauda, beginning a four-year relationship with Ferrari that was to contribute to a period of inspired technical reaffirmation for the Italian team. But even more important was the engagement of Luca Montezemolo as team manager, reporting directly to Enzo Ferrari himself. Montezemolo was a 25-year-old law student, extremely intelligent and with experience on the Lancia rally team. He was able to do the one thing that seems to be so difficult within the highly-charged Ferrari organization: keep the many members of the team—engineers, technicians, mechanics and drivers—working together in productive harmony. For Scuderia Ferrari, 1974 was the turn-around year. Since then, allowing for the inevitable problems that occur to every team in racing, Ferrari has been continually effective in Formula 1.

During the winter of 1973-74 the 312 B3 underwent an intense development program, resulting in a car so thoroughly modified that its relationship to the B3 of early 1973 was invisible, though traceable through various stages. With respect to the late-1973 B3 S, the new design for 1974 had one major and numerous minor changes. The main difference was a new monocoque with the driving position moved well forward and a supplementary fuel tank located between the seat and the engine; this concentrated the weight more toward the front. The new driving position resulted in a more upright cockpit fairing, while the air intake above the rollbar now had a ver-

New driver for Ferrari in 1974 was Austrian Niki Lauda, shown here at Fiorano in March beside latest B3, now with vertical scoop.

tical rather than horizontal scoop (initially this had a somewhat makeshift appearance but a later cowling covered the rollbar and the radius rods and blended the air scoop in handsomely). The front wing was similar to that of the B3 S, with the supports on the upper as well as lower surfaces of the airfoil, but the leading edge was tapered. (Later, a simplified nose with underwing supports only, improved the front wing's efficiency.)

The rear suspension had parallel lower links in place of the reversed A-arms, and lower radius rods were employed once again. The rear wing was supported on a pylon that enclosed the transmission oil

Essentially the definitive version of the B3 appeared at Kyalami with faired-over rollbar, front wing above nose. Lauda started from pole; Regazzoni (shown) started sixth, retired.

*Ferrari dominated the Spanish Grand Prix,
qualifying first and third, finishing first and
second; Lauda had fastest lap with victory.*

*Regazzoni and Lauda lead at Monte Carlo; Clay
spun, recovering for fourth place, and Niki
dropped out with ignition trouble after leading.*

cooler; various rear airfoils were used during 1974 (it was becoming apparent that different types were called for on different circuits, rather than simply changing the incidence), including parallel leading and trailing edge, swept-forward leading edges and swept-back trailing edges.

In the first race of 1974 at Buenos Aires, Ferrari's revived professionalism was clear to all. The more experienced Regazzoni put his B3 on the front row and his younger teammate was a respectable eighth-fastest in his first Ferrari outing. The Austrian did even better in the race, finishing an excellent second. Regazzoni did not get away well at the flag, dropping to twentieth place on lap 1, but he recovered quickly, set the fastest lap and worked up to a third-place finish behind Lauda.

Lauda was quicker in practice at Interlagos, starting from row two, but he broke a wing support and retired on lap 3; Regazzoni once again set the fastest lap, driving to a solid second place. This put him in the lead for the World Championship, a position not enjoyed by a Ferrari driver since Andretti's victory at Kyalami in 1971.

In the non-championship event at Brands Hatch in March, Regazzoni and Lauda qualified second and third, and finished fifth and second respectively.

Borsari and Caliri ponder 312 B3 at Fiorano. Cockpit cowling and air scoop are one piece.

Lauda led Regazzoni to another Ferrari 1-2 in the 1974 Dutch Grand Prix at Zandvoort.

Lauda had led ex-Ferrari driver Ickx on the wet track, but a defective rear shock absorber slowed Lauda enough to let the Belgian's Lotus go through to win.

The 1974 South African race saw a Ferrari on the pole for the first of many times that year. Lauda led away at the start, stayed in front for eight laps, and then followed Carlos Reutemann's Brabham-Ford until four laps from the end, when the B3's ignition failed. Regazzoni had qualified sixth, and dropped out on lap 65, his oil pressure gone, so the results did not record Ferrari's increasing raceworthiness.

Victory At Last

DOMINANCE WAS ACHIEVED in the next race at Jarama. Lauda qualified on the pole, again led most of the way, set a lap record and scored a convincing victory for Maranello. Regazzoni headed the second row and drove to a second-place finish behind his fast-rising, superbly gifted "number two." The Swiss driver still led the championship, now just 1 point ahead of Lauda. Forghieri was vindicated and the B3 could now enter the record books as a winning chassis.

But it was to be a tough season against tough opponents, notably Emerson Fittipaldi, now driving for McLaren. The Brazilian had won his own national race at Interlagos and repeated the performance in Belgium, edging out Lauda by less than a half-second after a race-long duel. Regazzoni gave Ferrari their third pole position in a row and came in a satisfactory fourth. The championship points were now Fittipaldi 22, Lauda 21 and Regazzoni 19.

The Ferraris started side-by-side from the front row at Monte Carlo, Lauda qualifying 0.3 seconds faster than Regazzoni. Clay led Niki for twenty laps, but spun, dropping to fifth; Lauda stayed in front for twelve more laps, but once again was let down by ignition trouble. Regazzoni finished fourth, gaining three points that would keep him near the top of the championship table.

Transmissions put the Ferraris out at Anderstorp, but this was a Tyrrell circuit, Jody Scheckter and Patrick Depailler dominating practice and the results, and the 312 B3s did well to qualify third and fourth. But Scuderia Ferrari was in control again at Zandvoort, taking over the front row for the start and the first two places at the finish, Lauda heading Regazzoni by eight seconds. Nevertheless, Fittipaldi still led the title chase with 31 points, one more than Lauda and three ahead of Regazzoni.

The Ferrari drivers were in front again after the French Grand Prix at Dijon, although it was Ronnie Peterson who won that race for Lotus, ahead of Lauda and Regazzoni. Lauda qualified on the pole and led for sixteen laps until increasing tire vibration forced him to let Peterson through; Regazzoni qualified fourth fastest and although also troubled by tire vibration, ran in third position for the entire race. Points were Lauda 36, Regazzoni 32, Fittipaldi 31.

Then began a series of misfortunes, and mistakes, which kept the World Championship leader from scoring more than two points (even these contested) in the season's remaining six races. Although he was demonstrably the fastest driver in Formula 1, Niki Lauda was still lacking in the race craft that comes from long experience, which might have helped him avoid the troubles.

Unlucky Lauda

AT BRANDS HATCH, Lauda was simply unlucky. He did everything right—except win the race. He qualified for the pole, set the fastest lap and led for 69 of the 75 laps. But a deflating tire, caused by debris on the track, dropped him to second, then third. Perhaps he delayed his pit stop too long (if he had stopped immediately he might have got right back to second place) but at any rate after he did stop to change the tire he found the pit road blocked by an official course car, preventing him from rejoining the race! This circumstance was protested by the Ferrari team and after several weeks a tribunal awarded Lauda the 2 points for the fifth position he would have taken if he had got back on the circuit. But it was the puncture itself that had

61

Front and rear ends of 312 B3 at the Nurburgring.
Rear wing is well isolated on gearbox-mounted pylon.
Engine demounts as a unit from back of monocoque;
gearbox is longitudinal 5-speed with inboard brakes.
Regazzoni drove a superb race to win the 1974
German GP, take lead in World Championship.

Lauda led the Italian Grand Prix by a wide margin over the Brabhams of Reutemann and Pace but had an engine failure on lap 30.

Cowl air intakes tried on this B3 at Monza in 1974 anticipated shape of 1976 312 T2.

taken victory from him; this proved to be the turning point of the season. Regazzoni, who qualified seventh, took three points with a fourth-place finish.

At the Nürburgring, Lauda's own eagerness to go in front caused him to brake late for a corner, on the very first lap when his tires were not yet warm enough to give him the expected adhesion. This put him off the track and out of the race. He had qualified fastest, with Regazzoni right beside him, but had allowed Scheckter to get past him at the start. Regazzoni, on the other hand, drove a trouble-free race to victory, Ferrari's third of the season. He led every lap and re-established himself at the head

of the championship list, with 44 points to Scheckter's 41 and Fittipaldi's 37.

At the Östereichring, Lauda again qualified on the pole, but he could not match Reutemann's pace, lost power, and then a valve went after 17 laps. Regazzoni gained two points on his rivals by finishing fifth; his performance was better than that, though, as he ran second for many laps and also set the fastest lap.

At Monza, Ferrari was expected to win, with none other than Lauda again at the head of the starting grid. He and Regazzoni dominated most of the race, first the Austrian and then the Swiss leading, their superior speed partly the result of running thinner-section rear wings at reduced incidence, without giving up much downforce. It was the engines that let them down, Lauda's after 32 laps and Regazzoni's after 40. The next worst thing was that Fittipaldi gained six points with a second-place finish.

By qualifying on the pole at Mosport, Fittipaldi showed that he was not going to inherit the championship simply from Ferrari's misfortunes; he intended to race for the title. For the first 67 of the 80 laps, Lauda kept ahead of Fittipaldi, driving with steady command, until misfortune again put him off

Final unlucky blow for Lauda was to spin off on Watson's debris at Mosport, after leading Fittipaldi convincingly for 67 of 80 laps.

the track. He was the first driver to come upon a coating of dirt on the circuit, left by John Watson's crashed Brabham, and the Ferrari slid helplessly into a barrier. Fittipaldi won the race and tied Regazzoni, who finished second, for the point lead, at 52 apiece.

Regazzoni or Fittipaldi?

IT ALL CAME DOWN to the final race at Watkins Glen. Lauda's troubles had put him out of the running for the title, but either Regazzoni or Fittipaldi could become champion by beating the other. Surprisingly, neither driver was competitive in the U.S. race, the Brazilian qualifying eighth and the Swiss ninth, but Fittipaldi found his fourth-place finish sufficient for the championship as Regazzoni came in eleventh after pitting three times with front shock absorber trouble. The same problem kept Lauda from running higher than fourth and put him out altogether after 38 laps. Ferrari had lost a likely World Championship through an unexpected technical deficiency at the eleventh hour.

But the season was so much better than in 1973 that it had to be regarded as a success. Ferrari had come from the depths of despondency to the first rank, scoring three victories, ten pole positions and six fastest laps in fifteen championship events. Regazzoni was second in the driver's championship, Lauda fourth, and Ferrari runner up in the manufacturer's category. A good, if not outstanding, season that demonstrated the resiliency of the Ferrari organization.

This organization would gain the 1975 World Championship with the next of Forghieri's Formula 1 cars, the 312 T, as told in the following chapter. In the South American events, however, the 312 B3 had two more races to run before retirement. Ferrari seemed to have set these cars up for maximum reliability, going for points while the new 312 T was getting its final pre-race development, and in South America Lauda and Regazzoni were moderately competitive but not challengers for outright victory. The Austrian qualified fourth for both races, finishing sixth in Argentina and fifth in Brazil, while Regazzoni qualified seventh and fifth respectively, coming in fourth in both races. With these results, the 312 B3 concluded a long and difficult development, experiencing every level of competitiveness from hopeless to triumphant.

Monocoques of 312 B3 010 (engine installed) and 014 being rebuilt by Sport Auto, Modena, in 1976.

Chapter 6

312 T F1 Championship Racing Car

WHILE THE MANY VERSIONS of the 312 B3 had soldiered on, race after race, as Scuderia Ferrari rebuilt its organization to professional efficiency, the new 312 T was competitive almost right "out of the box," and won its second race. It was evolutionary in most respects, somewhat resembling the 312 B3 with a similarly shaped airbox, but it was a completely new chassis with one revolutionary feature, indicated in the new designation.

The letter T stood for *trasversale* and referred to the transverse 5-speed gearbox developed especially for the 1975 Formula 1 car. Some advantage was gained in weight distribution, the new layout concentrating more of it within the wheelbase, but the most important purpose was an efficient power flow, calculated to be as much as 20 percent better than with the longitudinal transmission. The boxer engine now produced an even 500 bhp at 12,200 rpm (although of course each individual racing engine varies in actual output), with a broader mid-range torque band, improving further its main advantage over the Ford Cosworth DVF.

The monocoque of the 312 T was designed to accommodate more efficiently all the components developed so laboriously on the 1974 B3, with a great concentration on the overall aerodynamics. The 312 T certainly looked more slippery than its stubby but purposeful predecessor; its nose was narrower and more tapered, allowing better airflow under the front wing, the water radiators were relocated so that their air exhausted out of the sides of the body, and long triangular intakes at each side led to the obliquely positioned oil radiators. Ahead of the rear tires the body panels swept upwards to lessen (minimally, of course) the aerodynamic disturbance caused by these huge Goodyears. All in all, the body of the 312 T was more of a wedge, with careful attention to clean airflow throughout, and the cars raced in 1975 showed even greater refinement over the prototype (018) in its original form as shown to the press late in 1974.

The front suspension had longer upper arms with angled coil spring/shock absorber units; in back, the parallel lower links were replaced by reversed A-arms and the lower radius rods were omitted. Track dimensions were nearly 10 cm narrower front and rear (now 1510 and 1530 mm respectively), with the wheelbase increased marginally to 2518 mm. New cast magnesium alloy wheels were supplied by ESAP; these were of modular rim design with a four-spoke center in front and a solid center disc in back. With the same smoothly-working organization and

Designation T (trasversale) denoted compact new transverse 5-speed gearbox.

the same two drivers as in 1974, Scuderia Ferrari and the 312 T were ready for 1975. Four additional chassis (021, 022, 023, 024) were constructed as development work continued on 018. The B3s gained useful points for Lauda and Regazzoni in the two South American races; for the South African race at Kyalami on March 1 there were two 312 Ts (018 and 021) ready to run, although a single B3 was taken along as a backup car for Lauda. Even though Clay was the more experienced driver and had come close to winning the 1974 World Championship, Niki was clearly the faster of the two on most occasions and was effectively if not nominally the team leader. It is to Regazzoni's great credit that he became the most generous and cooperative number two driver a team could want. And he was often ready to win when his team leader wasn't competitive.

Lauda qualified fourth fastest behind the Brabhams of Carlos Pace and Carlos Reutemann and the Tyrrell of Jody Scheckter; Regazzoni was less than three-tenths of a second slower but that put him ninth on the grid. In the race the Swiss made a much better start than the Austrian, running most of the race in fifth place until a throttle link failed. This let Lauda into fifth at the finish. Neither Ferrari had challenged for the lead, but it was a strong first outing for the 312 T.

*Prototype 312 T shown at Fiorano in 1974
had Regazzoni's name and number on one
side, Lauda's on the other.*

Regazzoni and Lauda in 312 T debut at Kyalami, 1975.

*Spare 312 T 018 with rain tires, sits between the
race cars of Lauda (022, number 12) and
Regazzoni (021, 11) at Barcelona in 1975.*

The *trasversale* was ready to win in the first European event, a non-championship race at Silverstone in England. Only Lauda was entered, but his 312 T (a new chassis, 022) qualified second and took him to a minor but significant victory. Ferrari superiority was obvious in the Spanish Grand Prix at Barcelona, but it was a race the Scuderia (and most of the other teams) would like to forget. Lauda and Regazzoni qualified 1-2 on the front row, but both went out on the first lap when Andretti's Parnelli hit Clay's 312 T and knocked it into Niki's. The race had been boycotted by several drivers because of inadequate safety precautions around the circuit, and it ended prematurely and tragically when the leading Embassy-Hill of Rolf Stommelen suffered a broken wing mount and crashed into the crowd, killing four spectators.

Three in a Row

BEGINNING AT MONTE CARLO, Lauda started a string of victories that made him the only likely candidate for the 1975 championship. He qualified on the pole in the Monaco race, which began on a wet track, and led for all but the one lap on which he stopped to change tires as the road dried. It was a convincing display of the new Ferrari domination, although Regazzoni made a poor start from sixth position and put his car out with front-end damage at the chicane on lap 36. Although Ferrari had enjoyed many victories on other circuits over the years, Lauda's win was the first for the team at Monte Carlo since 1955, twenty years before, when Maurice Trintignant won in a four-cylinder 625 F1.

Having found the winning habit, Lauda did it again at Zolder in Belgium. He qualified on the pole (Regazzoni was fourth) and followed Pace and Vittorio Brambilla for several laps before taking charge. Regazzoni went well, fighting back to fifth place and setting a lap record after dropping to tenth position when he stopped to change a blistered tire. Lauda's performance was convincing throughout, and even a broken exhaust pipe, which cost him some power near the end, didn't really endanger his lead. He was now ahead of Fittipaldi in the championship standings, 23 points to 21, and he was to stay at the top of the table for the rest of the season.

The Swedish race at Anderstorp didn't look promising for Ferrari (Lauda qualified only fifth and Regazzoni twelfth) but the result was a hat-trick for

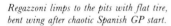

Regazzoni limps to the pits with flat tire, bent wing after chaotic Spanish GP start.

Monaco was first of three consecutive wins for Lauda and 312 T early in 1975.

Hunt got the best of Lauda at Zandvoort after gaining advantage during stops for rain tires.

Lauda out front was the story in nearly every race start in 1975; he leads at Paul Ricard, Nurburgring and Osterreichring in this series of photos, and is just headed by his teammate Regazzoni in championship-clincher at Monza.

Niki. He ran steadily as the front-runners fell back, one by one, and took the lead on lap 70, only ten from the finish. It was a case of Ferrari reliability earning a victory on a circuit where the 312 T chassis wasn't the best, but it was also a case of the driver doing everything possible with it. Surprisingly, he was even able to set the fastest lap. Regazzoni also ran steadily and was rewarded with third place.

At Zandvoort in Holland the Ferraris once again started from the front row but in the race they had to give way to the Hesketh of James Hunt, who held on to a 1-second lead over Lauda after taking the advantage following a spate of pit stops when all the competitors pulled in to change tires. Lauda set the fastest lap again, moving right up on the Englishman at the finish but unable to get by. Regazzoni was third, but almost a minute behind Lauda.

Lauda was at the front of the pack for the fifth time in six races at the Paul Ricard track in France. He got his revenge for Zandvoort by leading Hunt all the way, although his margin at the finish was less than 2 seconds as the Ferrari began to understeer toward the end of the 54-lap race. With his fourth championship victory in five 1975 mid-season Grands Prix, Lauda held such a commanding point lead that it was little more than mathematical possibility that gave his rivals any hope. On the other hand, Ricard was not a good result for Clay; he charged up to second place behind his teammate on lap 6 but the effort cost him an engine, one of only two failures the superb boxer unit was to suffer during the season.

Silverstone, a multiple-crash race won by Emerson Fittipaldi when his car was safely in the pits, was the first event since the multiple-crash Barcelona that a Ferrari did not earn any points. No less than thirteen of the twenty-six starters were involved in accidents in the rain, fortunately without tragic consequences; Lauda and Regazzoni were classified eighth and thirteenth and probably glad to leave the place in one piece. They had qualified third and fourth (just one-hundredth of a second apart) and Regazzoni had an initial spurt in the lead before the wind and rain put him off the track on lap 19 and he had to stop to replace the rear wing, dropping to next-to-last place. But he had already set the fastest lap, showing that the Ferrari 312 T was still the car to beat and that he could run ahead of Niki on occasion.

At the Nürburgring Niki made it clear who was the quickest driver in Formula 1 by setting the only under-7-minute qualifying time and leading convincingly for nine of the circuit's fourteen long laps. It was a front tire puncture that robbed him of almost certain victory; despite having to run nearly a half lap on the rim to get back to the pits for a new tire, he finished third and the 4 points put him very close to a certain title. Regazzoni, who had qualified fifth, set a lap record his seventh time around and was running second to Lauda when his engine's failing oil pressure made it blow up on lap 9.

Yet another rainy 1975 race was the Austrian

Regazzoni won his second Italian GP in 1975; less praiseworthy was Clay's performance at Watkins Glen, where he obstructed Fittipaldi (fist raised) before being black-flagged.

312 T, now carrying numbers 1 and 2, continued winning ways in 1976, Lauda taking first two events at Interlagos and Kyalami.

Grand Prix, stopped at mid point with zero visibility. The declared winner, Vittorio Brambilla in a March, had done a beautiful job of staying ahead of everybody during the race, crashing *after* he'd received the checkered flag! Because of the shortened distance, only half the regular ponts were awarded and Lauda got ½ a point for his sixth-place finish; this brought his total to 51½, exactly ½ point shy of the 18-point margin (over Reutemann) he needed to clinch the title in Austria. This was merely academic, delaying the official confirmation until Monza. At the Österreichring Niki had started from the pole again and led until lap 15 when his suspension settings could no longer cope with the ever-wetter track surface and he was passed by cars better adusted for that stage of the race. Regazzoni started fifth and finished seventh.

Clay was able to win his own national event, the non-championship Swiss Grand Prix, which was mainly remarkable for being held at Dijon in France, as automobile racing is not allowed under the laws of Switzerland! Although qualifying only third, he was a popular winner at the finish.

Lauda Champion

ITALIAN FRENZY was at a peak for Monza and the home team didn't let them down. Lauda qualified a predictable first and Regazzoni started right next to him on the front row. Clay was always good for one standout victory each season, and Monza was his from start to finish, including the fastest lap. Lauda ran second for 45 of the 52 laps; a broken rear shock caused oversteer and let Fittipaldi pass him. This spoiled a perfect Ferrari 1-2 but Lauda's third-place finish made him World Champion and the Italian fans went berserk, with two heroes to mob, chanting *Re-ga-zzo-ni! Re-ga-zzo-ni! Re-ga-zzo-ni!* and *Lau-da! Lau-da!*

*Composite view in arena at Long Beach shows
Regazzoni's winning 312 T 024 at left,
Lauda's second-place 023 in center and spare
T-car 022, with rain tires, at right.*

*Mechanics pushing Lauda's 312 T wait at cross-
walk; team manager Daniele Audetto is at extreme
left, capomeccanico Giulio Borsari in cockpit.*

After debut of T2, Ferrari lent 312 T 021 to Scuderia Everest for 1976 non-championship Silverstone race on April 11; driver Gian Carlo Martini started and finished tenth. Note Dino-type road wheels mounted on car in garage.

Niki made his championship form all the more convincing with another pole position and another flag-to-flag victory at Watkins Glen in New York in October. Regazzoni qualified a mediocre eleventh and was black-flagged for balking Fittipaldi's McLaren, which was running second to Lauda at the time. This was a very unpopular move, and quite unnecessary as Lauda was doing fine up front and was in any case already World Champion. Luca Montezemolo decided to call Clay in and withdraw the car, if only to show who was running the team in its championship year. In addition to Lauda's title, Ferrari won the Constructors Championship with 72½ points to Brabham's 54, scoring victories in six of the fourteen championship events as well as both of the non-championship races entered. Regazzoni finished fifth in the Drivers' Championship with 25 points.

For 1976 Ferrari SpA SEFAC started on top and the 312 T continued its winning ways while the 312 T2, unveiled at Fiorano in October 1975, was being readied for the beginning of the European season. A remarkably harmonious design, the 312 T underwent few changes during its racing development (only detail work in the interests of reliability, plus chassis tuning for circuit conditions, including a shorter wheelbase of 2505 mm) and the cars defended the championship with only one readily apparent change: they wore the numbers 1 and 2 in place of the 11 and 12 used by Ferrari in 1974-75.

Lauda carried number 1, of course, and he finished the first two 1976 events, at Interlagos and Kyalami, in that position. At Long Beach Clay Regazzoni was unbeatable, qualifying on the pole and showing his team leader the way around for once. Niki was second from lap 5 to the finish, building his 1976 points total handsomely. The 312 T ended its brilliant career on a perfect note: 1-2, and fastest lap, set by Regazzoni.

The first *trasversale* was one of the most successful Ferrari Formula 1 cars of all time, its record only bettered by the 500 F2 of 1952-53, an era when Ferrari had only minimal opposition. The 312 Ts contested seventeen races and won eleven of them, including the last six they competed in. They also scored two second places, four thirds, two fifths and a sixth, and five other finishes; of the seven retirements, only four were for mechanical reasons. No modern Formula 1 machine can touch this record.

Boxer engine and transverse gearbox for chassis 024 during restoration at Sport Auto in 1978.

Chapter 7

312 T2 F1 Near-Tragedy and Ultimate Triumph

CERTAINLY THE 312 T, as completely successful a car as Ferrari could have hoped for, was not in immediate need of replacement when its successor, the 312 T2, made its press debut at Fiorano in October 1975. But the new regulations for bodywork, to take effect with the first European Grand Prix event in Spain in May 1976, limited wing dimensions and brought an end to the tall airboxes that had become *de rigeur* on Formula 1 cars of the mid 1970s. At the same time that he coped with these necessary changes, Ing. Forghieri made two innovations, one radical and one merely curious, that transformed the appearance of the *trasversale* racing car. Neither was destined to be used in competition.

The novelties were found at each end of the prototype T2. In front, the tires had small "fenders," combination aerodynamic and brake-cooling aids, that turned with the wheels. At the back, the much narrower rear suspension was located by a device not seen on a Formula 1 Ferrari since the front-engine cars of the 1950s: a De Dion tubular structure linking the two hubs. With modern circuits becoming

smoother, Forghieri believed that the device would give a great advantage in traction; in practice, this advantage was not consistent enough to reduce lap times, but Ferrari continued to experiment with the system well into 1976.

As revealed to the press, the prototype T2 carried number 1 and the name Lauda on the left side, and number 2 and the name Regazzoni on the right. While the monocoque and the radiator ducting along the flanks were generally similar to the 312 T, the cockpit cover had a completely different shape; gone was the tall airbox above the rollbar and replacing it were two NACA-type scoops ahead of the windscreen, ducting air along each side of the cockpit to the two boxes of six fuel-injection trumpets. Although the shape of these scoops was to undergo continual revision, they were characteristic of the entire T2 series.

The narrow track dimensions of the prototype T2 (1400 mm front and 1430 rear, respectively 110 and 100 less than on the 312 T) were not employed when the first raceworthy T2, also lacking the "fenders"

and De Dion rear suspension, made its debut in the non-championship event at Brands Hatch in March 1976. In fact, except for the slightly longer wheelbase (2560 mm on the T2 vs. 2518/2505 on the T), the revised cockpit aerodynamics made necessary by the new rules, and a minimally-revised monocoque, the 1976 312 T2 was very little changed from the T.

As related in the previous chapter, the 312 T served gloriously to the end, winning the first three 1976 World Championship races and giving Ferrari and Lauda a seemingly uncatchable head start. Even though Daniele Audetto replaced Montezemolo as team manager, it looked like 1975 all over again. The debut of the T2 was promising if unrewarding; Lauda qualified his single Brands Hatch entry second but retired on lap 17 with a fractured brake pipe. In its first championship event at Jarama the T2 led for 31 laps until passed by James Hunt's McLaren; Lauda, slightly injured in a tractor accident in Austria a few weeks before the race, was in pain and unable to maintain the initial pace. Regazzoni in the second T2 had worked up to the fifth place but lost five places after pitting to fix a leaking fuel gauge. But the sensation of the race, one of a series of squabbles, technicalities and near-tragedies that made 1976 a most unsatisfactory season, was the disqualification of Hunt's car for a wing-width infringement. This gave Lauda a temporary victory, later reclaimed for Hunt by an FIA tribunal, and the Austrian champion went on to score two further vic-

Meeting 1976 rules limiting wing size and eliminating air scoops, prototype 312 T2 with De Dion rear suspension, narrow track and front "fenders" was shown to the press in October 1975. Regazzoni, Ferrari and Lauda pose with it.

Lauda was declared winner of Spanish GP when Hunt's McLaren was disqualified but Englishman was reinstated later after a tribunal.

There were no doubts at Zolder; Lauda qualified fastest, set fastest lap and won. Teammate Regazzoni qualified and finished second in number 2.

Lauda again dominated the race at Monte Carlo, looking unassailable for 1976 championship.

Scoop tried at Zolder and front "fenders" at
Paul Ricard were among mid-season experiments.
Latter were banned as exceeding maximum width
on full lock; similar scoop reappeared in 1977.

tories in succession for the 312 T2, giving Ferrari a
nearly unprecedented six-for-six in the first part of
the season and himself a solid point advantage. Even
when Hunt's Spanish GP points were restored to
him the first week in July, and the gap narrowed by
12 points, Lauda still seemed unassailable.

After Spain, Ferrari went to Zolder in Belgium
and the T2s took the two front-row grid positions
and drove away to a 1-2 finish, Lauda adding the
fastest lap to a perfect flag-to-flag drive. Hunt split
the Ferraris for a few laps but his transmission let
him down and Regazzoni was right behind his team
leader for the rest of the way. Again at Monte Carlo
the T2s headed the grid and again Lauda led the entire race and took the fastest lap. Regazzoni ran third
for a while, dropped to fourth and then tore the nose
off his T2 on lap 73 when he was back in third and
closing rapidly on Jody Scheckter's 6-wheeled Tyrrell
P34 for second. Although Clay was uninjured, the
accident spoiled what could have been another Ferrari 1-2.

If everything had gone Lauda's way in the first
five months of 1976, things began to go slightly and
then disastrously wrong for him for the remainder of
the season. At Anderstorp, always a difficult track for
Ferrari, the T2s were simply uncompetitive and
Lauda was quite happy to take home 4 points for
third place, and Regazzoni 1 point for sixth. Hunt
qualified on the pole for the French Grand Prix at
Paul Ricard; Lauda stayed ahead of him for eight
laps until the Ferrari's engine seized (ending a
remarkable run of seventeen consecutive finishes for
Lauda) and Hunt went on to win. With the Englishman picking up another 9 points the same week from
his Jarama reinstatement, and Lauda losing 3, the
McLaren menace was just beginning to be felt.

The British GP at Brands Hatch was the second
debacle of 1976. A first-lap accident (triggered by
Regazzoni's spinning T2) caused a re-start and once
again Hunt's victory was cancelled out on a
technicality: his car had been repaired before the
"second" race was flagged off and this disqualified
him, the demotion being ultimately upheld despite
McLaren's strenuous protests. In the race itself
Lauda led for 44 laps before giving way to Hunt and
hanging on for second. With Hunt's disqualification,
Lauda led him on points 61 to 26 (although the final
decision affecting these standings was not made for
some weeks), Scheckter lying second at that point
with 29 points.

Lauda's Fateful Crash

THEN CAME LAUDA's near-fatal accident at the Nürburgring. It occurred on his second lap and it was
later disputed whether the crash was a result of car
failure or driver error; however, it was almost certainly the result of poor tire adhesion (Niki was using
slicks) on the alternately wet and dry circuit. Lauda
was pulled from the flaming cockpit by the combined
efforts of his fellow drivers Brett Lunger, Guy Ed-
wards, Harald Ertl and Arturo Merzario. Alive but
badly burned and in grave condition, Lauda was
given a fifty-fifty chance of survival and no chance of
ever driving again. That he fought back from near-
death to drive at Monza only six weeks later is an
often-told but still incredible story.

Following the accident, Ferrari sent no cars to the
Austrian event two weeks later. While obviously a
mark of respect to their hospitalized team leader, this
was a tactical mistake on the part of the Ferrari staff
because Regazzoni might have been able to reduce

Regazzoni precipitated a multiple-car accident
which required a restart for British Grand Prix.
Lauda "won" after Hunt was again disqualified.

Last Formula 1 race on the Nurburgring and
nearly the last race ever for Niki Lauda.

Hunt's point score (3, for fourth place) if he had driven at the Österreichring. When Ferrari did send Clay to Zandvoort, he qualified fifth (the car obviously suffering from the lack of Lauda's development testing) but drove a superb race to finish second, just nine-tenths of a second behind Hunt's McLaren.

Lauda's return to competition at Monza in September was somewhat awkward for Scuderia Ferrari, which had engaged Carlos Reutemann, a defector from the Brabham team, to replace him, so three cars were run. (The ultimate result of Reutemann's signing and Lauda's unexpected recovery was that Regazzoni, always a loyal and effective Ferrari driver, was dropped from the 1977 team, a most unpopular decision.) In the weeks preceding Monza, Lauda had repeatedly telephoned his regular mechanic Ermanno Cuoghi to request the most thorough car preparation. He qualified fifth, two places ahead of Reutemann and four ahead of Regazzoni, and after a mediocre start drove to a heroic fourth place. Regazzoni drove extremely well to take second behind Ronnie Peterson's March, and

Lauda amazed everyone with recovery and fourth-place finish at Monza. Regazzoni was second and Reutemann, recruited to replace Lauda, finished ninth in third 312 T2, number 35.

Reutemann was a distant ninth although he had run ahead of Clay for the first two laps. James Hunt was the victim of yet another debacle, this one over the octane rating of his fuel, and he had to start from the back of the pack, along with John Watson and Jochen Mass, as a result of their practice times being disallowed. In the race he spun off trying to work through the field, but the situation smacked of cheap politics on the part of the Italian organizers. Following Monza, the point standings (though not confirmed for another week) were Lauda 64, Hunt 47.

With Lauda still not back to his former expertise and the Ferrari 312 T2 missing the precious six weeks of development time, Hunt scored two wins in a row in North America. Lauda was eighth and pointless at Mosport because of an oversteer-inducing rear suspension malady, but ran a good third at Watkins Glen to stay ahead of Hunt on points, 68 to 65. It all came down to the Japanese GP, with yet another fiasco, in a season of fiascos, playing the major role.

A Calculated Decision

THE RAIN WAS SO INTENSE in the Fuji race that visibility was near zero. Lauda, having already been close enough to death for one season, made his much-criticized decision to withdraw from the race and Hunt went on to a third-place finish, 4 championship points and a 1-point margin over Lauda for the season's total. The year 1976 was a cruel one, often

for Hunt and ultimately for Lauda, but Ferrari was somewhat consoled by another constructor's title, the 312 T2 (helped by the 312 T) outpointing McLaren 83 to 74.

With Reutemann signed for 1977, the Lauda-Regazzoni-Ferrari combination, as nearly perfect a team as ever existed, came to an end. Lauda's withdrawal from the Japanese race, while never openly criticized by Enzo Ferrari, had a subtle negative effect on his standing in the team and Niki had to fight for all he was worth to assert his leadership. His success in doing so, and his second World Championship, resulted as much from hard-headed, dogged professionalism as from his undoubted driving skill.

For 1977 the 312 T2 underwent a number of detail refinements, most of them aerodynamic. Behind the scenes an exhaustive testing program involving countless modifications was at the heart of Ferrari's continued competitiveness in the face of tough opposition. The De Dion rear suspension had been thoroughly tested early in 1976 but as Niki Lauda commented, it was "Good, but not better" than the fully-independent design. The front "fender" brake scoops were used in practice for the 1976 French GP but were declared illegal by the stewards; in any case, there was no significant advantage to them. Throughout the winter of 1976 and well into the 1977 season the T2 was tested with every conceivable type of wing, air scoop and side panel form; chassis experiments included De Dion *front* suspension and even Ferrari's own version of the 6-wheeler. Unlike Tyrrell's tandem "locomotive" front-wheel arrangement, the experimental T2 had double rear wheels, somewhat reminiscent of those on specialized hillclimb cars. Ferrari used the narrower front wheels and Goodyear tires for this purpose, but even these made the rear width excessive and illegal. The basic reason behind all the suspension experiments was Ferrari's dissatisfaction with Goodyear tires; it was felt that the American company wasn't cooperating in making rubber to suit the boxer Ferrari's special handling and torque characteristics. As a result, Michelin tires had been developed for and tested by Ferrari over a period of several years; the success of this project led to a contract to run the French tires beginning in 1978.

On the 312 T2s raced in 1977, the most notable changes from the 1976 cars were a further-forward driving position; a revised, more abrupt, cockpit cowling with different air intakes and a higher headrest fairing; higher rear tire fairings; and a redesigned rear wing mount. Later in the season the side panels were modified twice, the ultimate T2 having radiator air exhausting out the top rather than the sides of the panels, which now had longer rear-tire fairings beginning at mid-wheelbase. The front wing design, which had "come right" on the 312 T and was little changed since then, received triangular endplates in place of the previous airfoil

Lauda's third place at Watkins Glen kept narrow
point lead over Hunt, but the McLaren driver took
the title in Japan when Lauda withdrew. Pit
shot shows Regazzoni car having rain tires mounted.

Carlos Reutemann climbs the curb on the way to
victory in 1977 Brazilian GP at Interlagos.

Pit board shows Lauda's lead over Scheckter and
Hunt near end of South African GP; pieces from
Pryce's Shadow are wedged under the 312 T2.
Note much smaller air scoops used in 1977.

Lauda started from the pole and finished second at
Long Beach after a long battle with Scheckter and
Andretti, one of six second places he had in 1977.

A fine shot of Reutemann at Monte Carlo, where
he drove to third place behind his team leader.

Lauda's consistency gave him two more second places at Zolder and Silverstone. Side ducting was changed in mid-season, with water radiator air exiting at top of monocoque and longer fairings fitted ahead of taller rear tires.

shape. That the T2 design (basically still similar to the 312 T) was able to run competitively for a second season, and win another World Championship, was a tribute to all the hard work put in, this despite a worsening lack of rapport between Lauda and most of the Ferrari staff (*not* including his regular mechanic Cuoghi). Lauda especially had difficulty dealing with the 1977 team manager Roberto Nosetto, as well as feeling he was getting less consideration than Reutemann.

At Buenos Aires in January 1977, for the first time since Fiat took control of SpA Ferrari SEFAC, the parent firm was identified by decals on the sides of the cockpit. The two South American races favored Reutemann, the Argentine driver placing third in his own national event and winning the Brazilian race, while Lauda dropped out with engine trouble and placed third respectively. Lauda gained his first victory since the Nürburgring accident in the South African GP, running out front most of the way despite collecting some of the debris from the unfortunate Tom Pryce's Shadow, which hit a marshall with instantly fatal results for both the driver and the track worker. Because of the debris from the Shadow, the T2 overheated and lost oil pressure but somehow completed the last 25 laps in that condition—good luck for Lauda for a change. Reutemann was eighth.

The 1977 Long Beach race was an epic three-way battle for Scheckter (Wolf), Andretti (Lotus) and Lauda. The South African led all but the last four laps, when Andretti and then Lauda got by him, the Ferrari then moving to within eight-tenths of a second of the Lotus at the flag. Lauda qualified for the pole and made the fastest lap in the race but made his move too late. Nevertheless the 6 points for second made him equal to Scheckter at the head of the

championship table. Reutemann had a collision with Lunger on lap 12 and dropped out.

In Spain it was Reutemann's turn to run second to Andretti after qualifying fourth. Lauda qualified third but did not race, a recurrence of his 1976 rib injury (from the tractor accident early in that year) giving him too much pain to drive with. But he came back to finish second at Monte Carlo, 32 seconds ahead of Reutemann, and again at Zolder where Reutemann spun off, damaging the bodywork and rear wing.

The Swedish GP was not Lauda's race; he ran in midfield, dropping steadily back to retire on lap 47 with unmanageable handling. Reutemann also started in midfield but soldiered on to a decent third place on a track that has never liked Ferraris. At this point in the season Andretti's Lotus 78 was the class of the field and the American looked like a probable champion. His victory at Dijon emphasized this, and the T2s were a mediocre fifth and sixth, respectively Lauda and Reutemann. Yet Lauda's two points moved him to the top of the standings, a position he was to consolidate in the next four races.

At Silverstone Lauda was second again, and Reutemann fourteenth. Niki's victory at Hockenheim was especially sweet, because it was in the German GP the previous year that he had nearly been killed. His closest rival for the championship, now that Andretti had had two breakdowns in a row, was Scheckter, who qualified for the pole and led the first twelve laps. But Lauda took command on lap 13, drove convincingly to the finish, and enjoyed the fastest lap as well. Reutemann stressed Ferrari dependability with a fourth-place finish. Andretti had another engine failure at the Österreichring and Alan Jones won Shadow's only World Championship race

89

Although 312 T2 race cars had only evolutionary changes, radical experiments were carried on at Fiorano, including double rear tires, De Dion front suspension, 20-cm wheelbase extension behind engine, heavily modified cockpit cowling and side fairings, non-sliding skirts, horizontal front coil springs and aerodynamic fairings behind rear tires. None was raced, although sliding skirts were developed on 312 T3-T5.

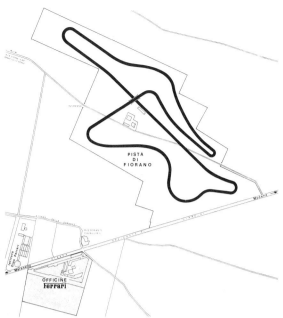

*By winning German GP at Hockenheim, Lauda made
up for 1976 misfortunes and neared 1977 title.*

*Lauda leads at start of Austrian Grand Prix;
at finish he was second yet again.*

On the victory rostrum at Zandvoort, Lauda is flanked by Jody Scheckter and Jacques Laffite.

Into and out of turn together, the 312 T2s of Reutemann and Lauda in the Italian GP.

Lauda's last race for Ferrari, at Watkins Glen, assured him of 1977 championship. Here he confers with Tomaini during practice as his head mechanic Cuoghi (who left team also) looks on.

93

*Gilles Villeneuve had brake trouble at Fuji,
later causing his T2 to run up over the back
of Peterson's Tyrrell and crash into crowd.*

Using Michelin tires, 312 T2's last race was a sensational victory for Reutemann in Brazil.

victory, but there was Lauda in second spot again, and Reutemann fourth.

At Zandvoort Lauda won his third race of 1977, leading for the last 56 laps and setting the lap record; Reutemann was sixth after running close behind Niki most of the way. Although the 312 T2 did not have the speed of the Lotus 78, its engine was far more reliable and it always ran near enough to the front to score highly at the finish. Yet another second place at Monza (his sixth of the season) all but clinched the title for Lauda, despite Andretti's victory; only Scheckter had a chance to tie his total score by winning all three of the last races. At Watkins Glen Lauda was fourth and Reutemann sixth and it was all over; the T2 had gained the World Championship for Lauda and its second straight constructor's title.

Lauda Moves On

THE END OF THE SEASON was anti-climactic. His title won, Lauda deserted Ferrari before the Canadian race, taking Cuoghi with him. This at least gave new recruit Gilles Villeneuve (signed as Reutemann's 1978 teammate) an extra drive but the Mosport event was not kind to either Ferrari driver; Reutemann retired without fuel pressure on lap 12 and the young Canadian lost a driveshaft on lap 76.

The concluding Japanese GP was even more unfortunate for Villeneuve, who lost his brakes, rode up over a rear wheel of Peterson's Tyrrell and was catapulted end over end into the crowd, killing two spectators and injuring several others seriously. Still strapped into the monocoque/engine unit, all that was left of the T2, Villeneuve survived unhurt. Reutemann drove a steady race, working up to second from a seventh-place start, bringing Ferrari's point total to a remarkable 95.

With the new 312 T3 not ready for the first two races of 1978, the T2 finished its long career wearing Michelin tires. As constructor's champions, the Ferraris might have deserved numbers 1 and 2, but Lauda took those with him to Brabham. In Argentina Reutemann qualified a strong second to the winner Andretti but finished seventh after dropping to fifteenth with a stop for tires. Villeneuve started seventh and finished eighth, yet was credited with the fastest lap. In Brazil Reutemann simply tore away from everyone at the start, leading all the way and scoring Michelin's first Grand Prix victory. Villeneuve got as high as fifth in the early laps but dropped back and then spun off after thirty-five laps. As had the 312 T before it, the 312 T2 ended its career with a victory, and Reutemann took fastest lap.

The 312 T2 was never an outstanding car but it was nearly always raceworthy and dependable. In thirty-two races from early 1976 through early 1978, it won eight of them, placed second twelve times, took seven thirds, four fourths, two fifths and five sixths. Not as brilliant a record as that of the 312 T, but nevertheless a fine one.

Above, Lorenzo Bandini's 512 F1, painted in blue and white NART colors at Watkins Glen in 1964; the boxer's debut ended after 57 laps with engine failure. Right, Peter Schetty in the 212 E Montagna at Freiburg-Schauinsland in 1969; he set the fastest time on every course that year and became European Mountain Champion. Below, Jacky Ickx' 312 B engine at Ontario in 1971. At that stage in its development the 3-liter Formula 1 boxer produced 460-470 bhp at 11,600-12,500 rpm.

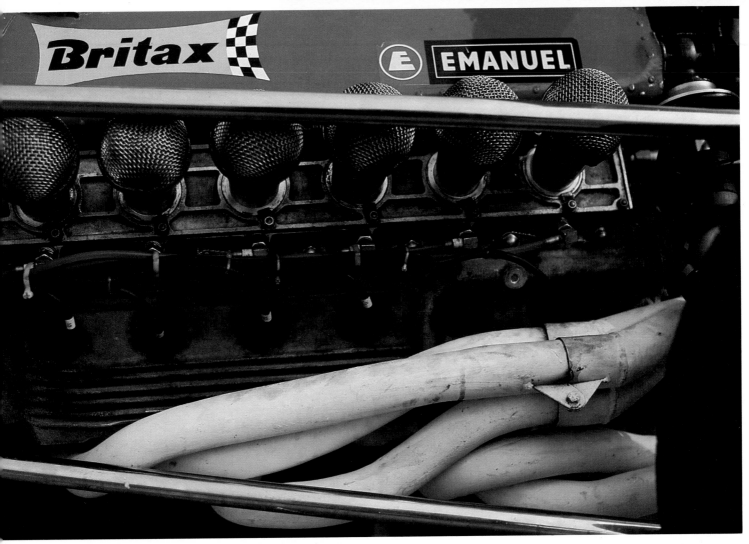

Above, Jacky Ickx in the 312 B2 winning the Dutch Grand Prix at Zandvoort in 1971; he had a long battle with the BRM of Pedro Rodriguez. Below, Clay Regazzoni in the 312 B3 at Monte Carlo in 1974; he started from the front row and led for 20 laps, but spun and finished fourth.

Above, Regazzoni's 312 T in the air at the Nürburgring, where he drove to a magnificent victory in 1975. Below, the Ferrari crew surrounds Carlos Reutemann's 312 T2 at Watkins Glen in 1977; in the race he came in fifth while his teammate Niki Lauda took fourth and his second title.

99

100

Design progression of Ferrari's Formula 1 boxers. Top to bottom, page 100: Mario Andretti, 312 B, Ontario 1971; Clay Regazzoni, 312 B2, Jarama 1972; Jacky Ickx, 312 B3, Paul Ricard 1973; Niki Lauda, 312 B3 S, Buenos Aires 1974; Lauda, 312 B3, Anderstorp 1974. This page: Regazzoni, 312 T, Zandvoort 1975; Lauda, 312 T2, Jarama 1976; Carlos Reutemann, 312 T2, Jarama 1977; Gilles Villeneuve, 312 T3, Watkins Glen 1978; Jody Scheckter, 312 T4, Zandvoort 1979. In its eleven years of competition the 3-liter boxer engine went from 455 to 515 bhp, powered cars to victory in thirty-seven World Championship races, and earned three Drivers' and four Constructors' titles for Scuderia Ferrari.

Left, Gilles Villeneuve and the 312 T3 in the rain at Montreal in 1978. Below, the engine of his 312 T4 at Long Beach in 1979. Bottom, he makes a valiant effort in the uncompetitive 312 T5 at the same circuit in 1980. Page 103 top, first lap at Sebring in 1972; Regazzoni's 312 PB (4) leads from Peterson (3) and an Alfa Romeo (31). Bottom, a production 365 GT Berlinetta Boxer in 1973.

103

Above, the Pozzi BB 512 of Ballot-Lena/Lafosse before the start of the 1978 Le Mans 24-hour race; they retired after 17 hours. Below, the Pozzi team in the pits at Le Mans in 1980. BB 512 LM number 76 finished tenth, driven by Dieudonné/Xhenceval/Regout; cars 75 and 77 retired.

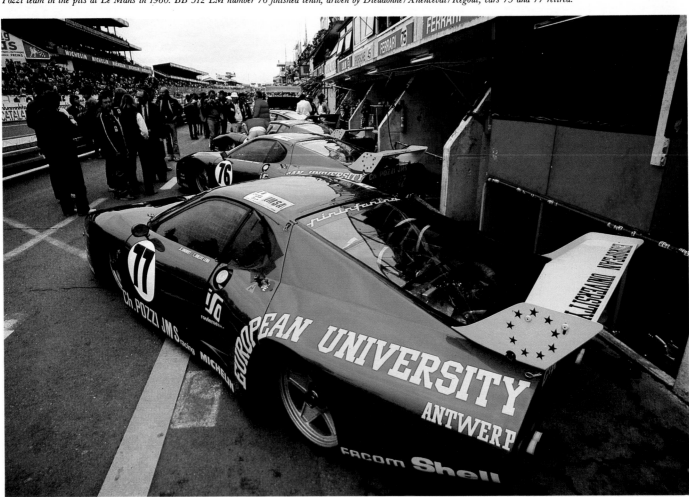

Chapter 8

312 T3 F1 Starting the Michelin Era

THE 312 T2 RAN ITS LAST two races, at the beginning of 1978, on the new Michelin tires. Honoring the last days of the old tire contract, its successor the 312 T3 had to be shown to the press with Goodyear rubber and decals when it made its debut in November 1977. But the T3 was developed with the new French tires and probably only ran a few laps at Fiorano on Goodyears for comparison.

Although a totally different machine, the T3 exhibited many of the details already tested on the ever-changing 1977 T2. These included the abbreviated headrest fairing, long side fences and top-exhausting water radiator outlets, but the T3 had a completely different appearance, its extremely tapered cockpit cowling accentuated by a sharply-pointed white stripe. Details seen on this T3 prototype (032) but soon changed were the shallow air intakes on top of the nose and the clear plastic mirror fairings blended into the windscreen. At its press debut 032 carried number 1—Ferrari *had* won the 1977 constructor's title as well as the Drivers' Championship with Lauda—but this number went to Lauda's Brabham for 1978 and the Ferraris reverted to the almost traditional 11 and 12.

The T3 had an adjustable wheelbase, between 2560 and 2700 mm, made possible by different sets of front A-arms, and the widest track dimensions yet: 1620 mm front and 1585 rear. Later a front track of 1700 mm was sometimes used, while the rear dimension was generally 1560. The 312 T2's weight had crept up to 590 kg, and the prototype T3's was quoted at 580, but this soon increased to an even 600

312 T3, wearing Goodyears because contract was still in effect, was unveiled to press inside Ferrari auditorium late in 1977.

New car was similar to T2 at back, much sleeker in front.

on the actual 1978 race cars. This was somewhat offset by an increased output from the boxer engine,
now giving 510 bhp at 12,200 rpm.

The Michelin tires had already been found to
reduce the T2's lap times by two full seconds at
Fiorano, and Reutemann achieved similar results at
Vallelunga. As mentioned in Chapter 7, he gave
Michelin a phenomenal first victory in the T2's final
race at Rio, but Goodyear was not sleeping and early
tests of its new compound were also dramatically improved. When Reutemann and Villeneuve raced T3s
for the first time at Kyalami they were only able to
qualify eighth and ninth fastest and in the race they
were eliminated by an accident and an oil leak
respectively.

Villeneuve Out Front

BUT AT LONG BEACH, always a good circuit for Ferrari
with the boxer engine's excellent mid-range torque,
the 312 T3s dominated the event, starting with the
two front-row grid positions. Gilles Villeneuve gave
the first really clear indication of his superb driving
ability and competitive spirit, leading easily for the
first 38 laps, but his exuberance led to a costly
mistake the next time around. Trying to lap Regazzoni's Shadow at an impossible point on the narrow
circuit (patience and the Ferrari's power would have
given him much easier places for this further along),
he hit the back of the Shadow and the T3 was
knocked into the wall and out of the race. But
Reutemann, running second at the time, drove
strongly to the finish to give the T3 its first victory
and Michelin's second.

This promising early form was soon to be put in the
shade by the performances of Andretti and Peterson
in the technically advanced Lotus 79, the first of the
super-efficient ground-effect "wing" chassis. At
Monte Carlo, Reutemann qualified on the pole but
made a mess of the start, was tapped by Lauda's

*Reutemann and Villeneuve test 312 T3 at
Fiorano with modified radiator ducting in
and under nose, different oil radiator outlets.*

Brabham, pitted the next time around and finished a
disappointed eighth. Villeneuve started eighth and
had moved up to fourth when his left front tire went
down as he entered the tunnel on lap 63; he exited
on three wheels and managed to come to a stop
without injury. The winner of the race was Patrick
Depailler, scoring a popular, long overdue first victory in his Tyrrell.

Then the Lotus 79s got in stride, Andretti and
Peterson taking two consecutive 1-2s at Zolder and
Jarama. The Ferraris qualified decently in both
races, Reutemann and Villeneuve finishing third and
fourth in Belgium but scoring no points in Spain
(Reutemann had an accident on lap 58 and
Villeneuve finished tenth after a stop for fresh
Michelins). The Canadian had been the only driver
to challenge the Lotus at Zolder, running a strong
second to Andretti while the T3's original set of
Michelins lasted. It was becoming apparent that in
addition to the pace of its rival the Lotus 79, the
Ferrari team was troubled by the erratic performance
of the Michelin tires, often good for competitive laps
but usually not lasting for a full race. Sweden saw a
further demonstration of this; Reutemann and
Villeneuve worked up to fourth and fifth positions
but ended up ninth and tenth (in reverse order) after

stops for new rubber. The Anderstorp race was notable for the victory of Lauda's fan-assisted ground-effect Brabham, later outlawed but the win being allowed to stand.

At Paul Ricard, Ferrari fortunes were at low ebb, the T3s dropping to the very tail of the field in mid-race. Michelin decided at least to use the event for experiments with different compounds, sending Reutemann out on a set of tires with which he was able to record the fastest lap at 1:48.56, almost as fast as his qualifying time.

The Lotus pair dominated the initial laps of Brands Hatch, but when they dropped out with engine troubles it was Carlos Reutemann who seized the lead by making a very quick pass on Lauda as they were lapping Bruno Giacomelli's McLaren. Carlos

went on to his third victory of the season; Villeneuve quit with a broken driveshaft, never really being in contention, but neither T3 driver had tire troubles. At Brands, a new side panel design, with the oil radiator air no longer exhausting at the top of the fairings, made its first appearance.

Three successive Lotus victories at Hockenheim, Österreichring and Zandvoort established Andretti and Peterson in unassailable 1-2 championship positions, with the Ferraris qualifying fairly well but scoring few points. In mid-season the T3's suspension was revised to suit the taller Michelin front tires; these gave quicker times but the French rubber was still only competitive on clean surfaces for short distances.

T3 in Skirts

DURING THE SUMMER Ferrari experimented continually with skirts in attempt to bridge the gap in handling established by the Lotus wing-car chassis. Outsiders doubted that the wider boxer engine would give enough area for real ground effect, but substantial gains were made on the T3 chassis and the design of the T4 for 1979 would show little disadvantage in this area compared to the Ford Cosworth V-8

Italian driver Elio de Angelis tries the 312 T3 at Fiorano in January 1978.

Villeneuve's T3 (shown) led for many laps at Long Beach but it was Carlos Reutemann who won the race.

Villeneuve's left front Michelin let him down at Zolder while he was running second; with new tires he moved back up to finish fourth.

Reutemann tests 312 T3 with skirts, modified flanks and radiator scoops at Fiorano in June 1978.

Reutemann won British GP after snatching lead from Lauda's Brabham. Michelin man approved.

powered cars. The skirts first appeared on the T3 at Monza, where Villeneuve delighted the Italian crowd by qualifying on the front row next to Andretti. These two drivers dominated the race, but it was a chaotic, tragic event, with Ronnie Peterson having a fatal crash on the first lap and Andretti and Villeneuve each being penalized a full minute for jumping the restart. Gilles led for 34 laps of the restarted race, finally yielding to Andretti, who led the last six laps and took the checkered flag. But after their one-minute penalties were imposed, they were classified sixth and seventh, a most unsatisfactory result capping a bad weekend. Reutemann

Further skirt tests were done on 312 T3 by Villeneuve at Fiorano in September 1978.

Ferraris passed Andretti after start of United States GP, ran 1-2 for many laps. Reutemann was the winner after Villeneuve's engine quit.

Villeneuve's long-deserved first victory came, appropriately, in his own national Grand Prix at Montreal. His wife Joanne looks on as he receives winner's trophy from Pierre Trudeau.

finished fifth on the road and was elevated to third by the reclassification. The ''lucky,'' official winner of the race was Lauda; both of the Brabham-Alfa Romeo's two victories were thus obtained under disputed circumstances.

The 312 T3 went to North America, where Michelin success was important to the company's prestige in a developing market, in a very strong position. The chassis was working well and the latest tires had become competitive. The Lotuses were still the cars to beat, Jean-Pierre Jarier becoming Andretti's very capable teammate after the death of Peterson, but the Ferraris showed the most real speed since Long Beach. Reutemann qualified second next to Andretti and Villeneuve was right behind Carlos in fourth. Both T3s pressed Andretti's ill-handling car from the start of the race and Reutemann went into the lead on the third lap, staying there to the finish. Villeneuve was right behind him until lap 23 when his engine gave out.

The Canadian scored a popular first victory in his own national event at Montreal, although it was Jarier who qualified fastest and led for 49 of the 70 laps. Villeneuve fought his way past Jody Scheckter's Wolf one-third of the way into the race and was sitting second when Jarier dropped out with an oil leak. With Scheckter (Ferrari's newly-signed driver for the following year) in second and Reutemann third, Scuderia Ferrari looked to be back on form. The 312 T3 had won four races in 1978; adding that of the T2 at Rio, Ferrari and Michelin had a successful if not outstanding first year together.

Forghieri on the 312 T3

WHILE THE T3 did not fulfill the promise shown at Long Beach, and only became consistently competitive at the end of 1978, the comments of Ing. Forghieri at the earlier U.S. race are nevertheless interesting, showing the kinds of problems a Formula 1 designer must face:

''The new T3 is a logical development of the T2, although structurally it is very different. The chassis is easier to build and also less expensive to build, and is different from our usual system in that it is built in two distinct sections—the central tub (a steel tube frame on which an alloy skin is riveted) and the two side sections, which are less stiff.

''The concept of the car is to ensure that the individual components do not compromise one another. Aerodynamically, for example, we now have much more freedom; we are able to make changes without upsetting the mechanical side of the car. What you see on the car at the moment is just one possible aerodynamic set-up. In the wind tunnel [Pininfarina's] we have already tried three others. And, in this vein, two engine inlet positions have also been used—one with two slots on top of the chassis, the other with ducts behind the front suspension.

''The engine and gearbox are also structurally different. We have new water pipe castings on the engine and two separate new castings on the gearbox, enabling us to mount top links directly on the gearbox and to run a lower center of gravity.''

For the first two races of 1979, in South America, the 312 T3 was still Ferrari's weapon while the T4 received its final testing in preparation for the South African GP debut. Jacques Laffite's Ligier was dominant at Buenos Aires and Interlagos; the Ferraris were not competitive at the Argentine track, failing to score any points, and did a little better in Brazil, Villeneuve taking fifth place and new-man Scheckter sixth. But both drivers had reason to be confident about the new T4 and Villeneuve even won the T3's final race, a non-championship event at Brands Hatch, for which no T4 was made available.

Chapter 9

312 T4 & T5 F1 **Front Runner and Back Marker**

ENZO FERRARI HIMSELF called the 312 T4 the ugliest Formula 1 car he had ever produced, but winners have a habit of looking good and the T4's unconventional shape seemed logically functional from the moment of its first-time-out 1-2 victory at Kyalami in March 1979. At its press debut in January it had simply looked weird. As Ferrari's first contender to be designed from the start as a wing car, it had the slab-sided, skirted mid-section that was pretty much the standard layout for the modern Grand Prix car. Ahead of the front suspension, however, the air flow was begun by a protruding leading edge, with the familiar Ferrari front wing attached below by a small nose cone. Given a driving position already as far forward as possible, and a cockpit cowling that angled sharply forward at the back, the overall impression was of a car that was trying to pass itself; in its first several races, and for most of the 1979 season before the Williams FW 07 became fully competitive, there were seldom any other cars in front of it!

The 312 T3 had been competitive at the end of 1978, even though its skirts had been a compromise, but Grand Prix experts did not expect Ferrari to be able to produce a truly effective wing car around the wide boxer engine, which intruded on the space required for air flow at the back of the chassis. The 312 T4 proved them wrong, at least temporarily, for there was to be enough downforce, combined with Ferrari's fabled torque, to make it the best Formula 1 car of 1979. In the long run the ultimate development of the wing concept, as exemplified by the Williams FW 07B, the Brabham BT 49 and the Ligier JS 11/15 (all Ford-Cosworth DFV powered), created a level of ultra-high-speed cornering in which Ferrari torque and Villeneuve wizardry could not make up for a significantly lesser amount of downforce, and the 312 T5 was to have a season as miserable as the T4's was triumphant.

The South African driver Jody Scheckter, once the *enfant terrible* of Grand Prix pilots but by 1979 a seasoned professional, was hired as Ferrari's number

First Ferrari designed as a wing car was the 312 T4, unveiled on January 15, 1979.

one. He made it clear that he had signed for the definite purpose of becoming World Champion, and that the Scuderia was the team he thought the best able to bring about this goal. In many ways the beginning of 1979 was like the positive reorganization of the Ferrari team that had occurred in 1974; there was a new driver, a new car and an atmosphere of solid confidence. Gilles Villeneuve, already a "veteran" of a full season with the team and the winner of the final race of 1978, was certainly the fastest number two driver in the business.

So fast was Villeneuve that he won the T4's debut race at Kyalami, stealing Scheckter's thunder in his home Grand Prix, as well as the next race at Long Beach. Jabouille's Renault turbo started from the pole in South Africa but Villeneuve qualified fastest for the U.S. GP West and set the fastest laps in both races. Scheckter finished second each time to give the T4 perfect 1-2 performances in its initial outings. The rest of the season was not to be so easy for Ferrari, but the cars delivered solid performances throughout the year to maintain the early lead. At Long Beach in practice both drivers tried out a different rear wing design, with the airfoil mounted ahead of the rear suspension instead of far to the back; the effect of the forward-placed wing was to make the car more "nervous," i.e. less stable but more usable. In the race Villeneuve used the regular rear-mounted wing and Scheckter the "bob-tail" ar-

rangement. After Long Beach Villeneuve had a two-point lead in the World Championship.

Scheckter Takes Charge

IF PERTURBED by his younger teammate's brilliance at the start of the season, Scheckter did not show it. He had been accumulating substantial championship points and he added three more by finishing fourth in the first European event, the Spanish Grand Prix at Jarama. The race was dominated by the Ligier team, with Patrick Depailler leading from start to finish. Villeneuve, who had also won the non-championship Brands Hatch race in the T3's final appearance, didn't maintain form in Spain; he got out of shape twice in attempted passing maneuvers and ended up seventh. He did achieve the fastest race lap, however, and still shared the championship lead with Depailler, at 20 points each.

Scheckter scored his first victory for Ferrari at Zolder in Belgium, also setting the T4's fourth consecutive fastest lap. But he did not dominate the race, led initially by Depailler and then Alan Jones' Williams, and only took the lead from Jacques Laffite's Ligier on lap 54. Villeneuve had been forced to drive right up over Regazzoni's Williams in an accident on the first lap; restarting last with a replacement nose cone, Gilles finished seventh again, out of the points but a very respectable result. Scheckter

New team leader Jody Scheckter tests T4 at Fiorano with regular and "nervous" rear wings, the latter for twisty circuits; note number "11½" resulting from use of Gilles' cowling.

Ferrari — DISTINTA LAVORI DA ESEGUIRE

VETTURA F1-312 T. N° TELAIO *037* N° GARA — GARA —

LUOGO — *LONG BEACH* — DATA — *7-4-79*

L'AVORI DA ESEGUIRE PER — DEL GIORNO — ORE

PERSONALE ADDETTO ALLA VETTURA — LAVORO ESEGUITO.

SPECIALISTI —

CONSUMO BENZINA	BENZINA MESSA	BENZINA RESIDUA	BENZINA CONSUMATA	GIRI EFFETTUATI	Lt / GIRO	Lt / 100 Km.

	ANTERIORE			POSTERIORE		
	ALTEZZA DA TERRA	CAMBER	CONVER.	ALTEZZA DA TERRA	CAMBER	CONVER.
CONTROLLO ASSETTO	+30			+30		
	STAT.			STAT.		
	-30			-30		

AMMORTIZZATORI	ANTER.	COMPRESSIONE —	POSTER.	COMPRESSIONE —
		ESTENSIONE —		ESTENSIONE —

RAPPORTI CAMBIO C/C	1ª	2ª	3ª	4ª	5ª	RUOTE MONTATE PER.	
MONTATI		14/32			21/29	ANT. TIPO.	POST. TIPO.
DA MONTARE		14/32			20/32	ANT. DEST. / ANT. SINIS.	POST. DEST. / POST. SINIS.

X) Fare rodaggio

X) Togliere ammortizz. per controllo -5 10°/65°

X) Motore N° 46 con pompa a 8 bulb.

X) Semiasse 13 - 14

.) Bandelle MIKI con cordon. sul tetto

X) Con Km 16 dietro

X) Pastiglie rodate

.) Aiuto aerodinamico come fine prove

.) Riposiz. carrozz. dietro pop[p]iatosto

.) Sistemare riscaldatore olio

X) Cont. radiatore olio **3 P/6 A**

X) Riparaz. freni - cont. ture sul tubec.

X) Cont. ture pattini e freno

X) Cont. tubo flessibile freni

NOTE: .) Benzina 150

VISTO DEL CAPO MECCANICO A LAVORI ESEGUITI.

OM - A 4 210 x 297 mm

Check sheet (for Villeneuve's car 037 at Long Beach) gives list of adjustments and modifications to make during Saturday practice; they worked!

At Long Beach Villeneuve repeated his convincing Kyalami victory and Scheckter was again second, giving T4 perfect start toward championship. Scheckter practiced with regular rear wing but used "nervous" type in the race.

now led the World Championhip on points, though shared with Laffite at 24.

Scheckter scored *his* second consecutive win at Monte Carlo, this time qualifying for the pole, dominating the race and moving into a clear championship lead. Monte Carlo was another circuit, like Long Beach, on which Ferrari torque was unbeatable; Villeneuve ran second to his team leader for many laps before retiring with transmission failure. This may have been the result of his having run his wheels up over the curbs on occasion, something Scheckter had been careful to avoid. Despite the absolute speed one driver may be able to achieve, it

Scheckter tested several types of rear bodywork, designed to improve downforce, at Fiorano; note upswept fairings and skirts between rear tires.

Villeneuve the fighter: after leading first half of French GP until his Michelins went "off," he raced wheel-to-wheel with Arnoux for second.

Jody ahead of Gilles in British GP, where T4s were outclassed by Williams; note upswept exhaust pipes, angle of rear wing in hard cornering.

is usually a blend of good speed and the careful professionalism born of experience that wins championships. This was what Scheckter was bringing to bear in mid-1979. Both of the T4s had the forward-mounted rear wings at Monte Carlo.

First Turbo Victory

THE FRENCH GRAND PRIX at Dijon saw a popular and long overdue win for the Renault turbo in the hands of Jean-Pierre Jabouille. But it was Gilles Villeneuve who led the first half of the race and provided the drama by fighting wheel-to-wheel with René Arnoux's Renault for second place in the last several laps. The Ferrari took second, and the six points moved Villeneuve up to second in the World Championship behind Scheckter, who still led in spite of finishing only seventh and scoring no points at Dijon. Villeneuve and Arnoux were criticized for potentially dangerous driving, but they were entertaining the fans by *racing*, not just cruising to the finish in respectable positions. The British Grand Prix, on the very fast Silverstone circuit which favored the phenomenal adhesion of the Williams chassis, was the first race in which the 312 T4s were well off the pace; they qualified eleventh and thirteenth and Scheckter must have been happy to get two points from a fifth-place finish. Villeneuve had run right behind him for much of the race but stopped on lap 50 and then again on lap 63 with fuel vaporization trouble; he did not get going again but

was classified fourteenth on laps completed.

Hockenheim was another fast "Williams" circuit and again Scheckter did the professional thing by driving steadily into fourth place, Villeneuve ran behind him again, but the French Canadian's engine was off-song with an incorrect fuel mixture and he was further troubled by a collapsing rear wing. After getting it replaced, along with four fresh tires, he was able to go fast again, if only into eighth place, but at least achieved the fastest lap.

A third consecutive Williams win came at the Österreichring, but the Ferraris were more competitive, Villeneuve taking second and moving back into second position on the championship table (Laffite had gone ahead of him at Hockenheim), Scheckter taking fourth and maintaining a useful if not commanding points lead. By that part of the season the Williams and Renaults had established themselves as the fastest cars, the former on adhesion and reliability and the latter on power, with the Ferraris still fast enough to secure good finishing positions. This was evident at Zandvoort, where Scheckter took a crucial second place after qualifying only fifth fastest, and Villeneuve led in mid-race after starting only sixth. Villeneuve blew a tire on lap 49; his frantic drive back to the pits, first on a shredded tire and then on a bare rim, was again criticized as wild, but showed a fierce desire to compete unmatched by any other driver.

Another World Championship

THE WILLIAMS PARADE had gone on long enough, and a couple of mid-field Ferrari finishes at Monza wouldn't satisfy the Italian crowd, even if Scheckter's points lead was a healthy 51 to Villeneuve's 38 and the 36 of the nearest non-Ferrari driver, Laffite. The T4s didn't dominate practice but they ran 1-2 for most of the race, including the most important last lap; only Arnoux's Renault had got ahead of them in the race, and only for eleven laps. There hadn't been as satisfactory a Monza race, from the Italian point of view, since 1975, when Regazzoni won in a Ferrari 312 T and Lauda took the championship with a third-place finish. Villeneuve finished less than a half-second behind Scheckter in 1979, making it clear that he could have gone faster but was being a good boy, and a supportive number two. Almost from the moment of Scheckter's championship, a subtle understanding became recognized within the Scuderia: that Villeneuve was the faster driver and, having fulfilled his obligation as teammate in 1979, he became the team's unofficial number one from then on. A modified 312 T4, called the T4B, appeared in practice at Monza. It had a revised exhaust system and outboard-mounted, twin-caliper rear brakes, with slightly different rear body ducting as a result. Villeneuve drove the car (chassis 041 modified) in practice, but went faster in his standard car. Ferrari also clinched the Constructors' Championship; for

*Scheckter settled down, drove for championship
points in mid-season; here he drives to fourth
place in the Austrian GP at Osterreichring.*

the first time in the series, the performances of all a team's cars were scored, rather than just the highest-placed, and Ferrari's 95 points after Monza could not be matched with two races remaining, even if the second-placed Williams team were to score consecutive one-twos.

The victors went to Imola to entertain another Italian crowd in a non-championship event, which was being held to qualify the circuit for its 1980 championship status. With the 1979 titles won, and no points at stake anyway, the Ferrari team took two cars in T4B configuration (numbers 038 and 041) to Imola, qualifying for the two front-row positions. Scheckter finished third and Villeneuve took seventh and fastest lap.

The French Canadian was eager to repeat his 1978 home win at Montreal, and he did lead Jones for 50 of the 78 laps, but the Williams driver pressured him relentlessly before forcing past. There was tire contact, as had occurred between Villeneuve and Arnoux at Dijon; Gilles has never waved anyone by if his Ferrari was still raceworthy! Scheckter brought his T4 into fourth place.

Villeneuve got his revenge in the final 1979 race at Watkins Glen, qualifying third (Scheckter was sixteenth!) and leading for all but five of the race's 59 laps. It was Jones who got by him again in mid-race, but after both drivers had to stop for tire changes, one of the Australian's wheels, insufficiently tightened before he left the pits, came off and he was out of the race. Scheckter's retirement, from a puncture, was the first and only time in 1978 that his T4 failed to finish. Of the fifteen championship races, he ran two in the 312 T3 (being eliminated in an accident at Buenos Aires and finishing sixth at Interlagos) and scored points in eleven of his thirteen T4 starts. Cer-

tainly the most effective driver and car combination had been realized. By winning at Watkins Glen, Villeneuve equaled Scheckter's three wins and brought his point total up to 47, just 4 behind the champion's. The team's total was 113 (greater than the drivers' combined scorable total, as Scheckter had to drop 9 points and Villeneuve 6), besting Williams by 38. (Ironically, if the 15-race season had been split in two following the Dijon race rather than before it, the best-four-from-each-half system would have made Villeneuve the champion by two points! The actual result was just, if derived illogically.) It had been a Ferrari year, with the 312 T4 the car for the job.

From Best Season to Worst

THE FERRARI 312 T4 started out and ended up a winner. By not being entered in the first few races of a second season, as was usual practice for Ferrari, it was spared the ignominity that fell upon its successor, the 312 T5. The reasons why the team could go from champions to also-rans in a few months were at least three, none as surprising as they might have seemed at first. The basic fact of modern Grand Prix racing is that no chassis, no matter how well designed, has a development life sufficient to dominate two consecutive seasons. Secondly, no car could compete effectively in 1980 without a full ground-effect chassis, no matter how good its engine. And perhaps most significant, the Ferrari factory was hard at work on a totally new turbo car, the 126 C; despite the short-term advantages of putting more development effort into the boxer-engined T5, the long-term potential of the turbo design had to take precedence.

Was this in fact a foregone conclusion within the

*312 T4s of Scheckter and Villeneuve, here
ahead of Laffite's Ligier, dominated Italian GP,
taking 1-2 in race and World Championship.*

Ferrari team, even at the beginning of the year? Both drivers were probably frustrated by the T5's lack of competitiveness, but neither seemed surprised, much less bitter about it. In Scheckter's case, he was able to enjoy the financial rewards of being the reigning champion. For Villeneuve, the future potential of the 126 C was something to look forward to as he struggled fruitlessly with the T5. Characteristically, he drove the T5 for all it was worth; even if he had no hope of victory, he consistently tried for the next highest position in the field, certainly the attitude of a future champion.

Even though Ferrari had its worst Formula 1 season ever in 1980 (worse, incredibly, than the 1973 disaster), the 312 T5 was not a *bad* design. It was simply an ineffective interim car, one to campaign while Ferrari prepared for an entirely new era in Formula 1 racing with the new 1.5-liter, 120-degree V-6 Turbo engine. The T5 looked very much like the T4 but was in fact extensively redesigned, with different suspension and many detail changes throughout. The body looked very similar, except for different ducting out the tops of the side pods, and a vertical spine added to the back of the cockpit cowling.

Villeneuve showed his brilliance on the few occasions that the T5 was even moderately competitive (he qualified third in Brazil and actually led the first lap by virtue of a demon start), but he scored a grand total of only six points throughout 1980. Scheckter's results were even less impressive: two points from one fifth-place finish. If speed was lacking, most demoralizing was the lack of Ferrari's traditional reliability; only sixteen cars finished out of 27 starts. Perhaps the crowning blow was that the World Champion was unable to qualify for the Montreal race. But he qualified for his final race at Watkins Glen, finished tenth and ended his career on good terms with the team he'd given a championship the year before.

It would be pointless to detail the 1980 events race by race in this chapter; the performances of the T5 can be examined in the full Racing Record at the end of the book. Interestingly, no less than six T5s

were built, compared to five each of the T3 and T4. It is also surprising that the first of the new 126 C turbos should be numbered within the boxer sequence (047, between two T5s); certainly such a radical technical breakaway would have called for a new series. The first 126 C practiced at Imola in 1980, qualifying faster for Villeneuve than his regular T5, but its race debut was saved for 1981.

Will the boxer engine be used again in Formula 1? Ferrari himself suggested that it might still be more effective on certain circuits than the turbo. If so, will the T5 be further developed for the purpose or will we see a T6? The writer is inclined to believe that the present boxer engine series has run its course in Formula 1 and that if future boxers are employed they will be designed in direct response to the technical demands of the time.

The political situation in World Championship Formula 1 racing, involving at the time of writing a seeming battle to the death between the FISA and FOCA factions, is so confused that even a projection of who will race with whom (or if!) in 1981 cannot be predicted with any confidence. Ferrari has sided with FISA and the national sporting clubs which have traditionally sanctioned Formula 1, while the majority of the British-based teams using Cosworth-powered equipment are backing FOCA and its financial control of the World Championship. If there is ultimately a split, the future regulations for Formula 1, and thus the technical solutions, will be different from those that have been in force during the development of the Ferrari 312 B and T series.

Many observers of the Formula 1 scene have felt that the development of the wing principle has caused a regrettable decline in the amount of influence that driver skill can have on lap times, and that wing cars are simply not maneuverable enough to provide entertaining, sporting competition. The writer believes that when a driver of the caliber of Gilles Villeneuve is found struggling near the back of the field, this must be true. In any event, the turbo will supersede the long and technically inspired range of Ferrari boxer engines in Formula 1.

*Forghieri and Villeneuve open champagne at
debut of 312 T5 on November 26, 1979.
New car, basically a refined T4, gave Ferrari
its most uncompetitive season since 1973.*

*Compared to 1979 dominance, Ferrari worked hard
to qualify tenth and sixteenth at Long Beach in
1980; Scheckter inherited fifth place.*

*Ferrari mechanics set front wing on T5 at
Imola. Drivers destroyed one car each, Jody
in practice and Gilles in this spectacular
crash in race; fortunately he was unhurt.*

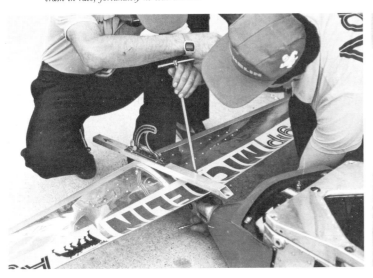

Chapter 10

$312\ PB$ **Ferrari's Greatest Sports/Racing Car**

IN 1970 THE FERRARI 512 S, a 5-liter V-12 contesting the Sports category in international endurance racing, had as its opponent the Porsche 917. Even though it was only marginally less fabulous than its German rival, the 512 S won only one race, the Sebring 12-hour event, and the Maranello engineers knew they were fighting an uphill battle. Revised 5-liter sports cars, designated 512 M, were entered in 1971 contests, but a totally new, much smaller 3-liter machine ran in the Prototype category in the same races. It had a boxer engine.

Officially called the 312 P (*Prototipo*), this car has come to be known as the 312 PB, the letter B identifying it as a boxer in contrast to the V-12 Prototypes raced in 1969. Testing of the new car began on the Modena circuit late in 1970 and it was revealed to the public at a factory press conference in December, along with drivers Mario Andretti, Ignazio Giunti, Arturo Merzario, Gianclaudio Regazzoni and Nino Vaccarella (the team's number one, Jacky Ickx, was not present). Compared to the massive 512 cars, the 312 PB looked tiny, with simple spyder bodywork following the inspiration of the ultra-short Porsche 908/3s that had raced in the Targa Florio and Nürburgring events in 1970. In effect, the 312 PB was a full-bodied Formula 1 car, using the engine, drive train and suspension of the 312 B single-seater. The chassis was the usual Ferrari tubular structure covered with sheet aluminum, while the bodywork was in two main sections, the front part including the forward-swinging doors. The wheelbase was only 2220 mm (87.5 inches) and the weight 585 kg (1290 pounds). The water radiators were mounted in the middle of the chassis on each side of the cockpit, with air intakes recessed into the doors, and the oil radiators sat above the engine.

The opening in the nose helped keep the front end down, the center duct having no cooling function, while the two small side ducts led to the front brakes. As tuned for long-distance racing, the 78.5 x 51.5-mm, 2991-cc flat-12 engine produced 440 bhp at 10,800 rpm, about 30 bhp below that of the current Formula 1 units. The gearbox was a 5-speed and a 120-liter (approximately 31.5-gallon) fuel tank was placed in the left side of the chassis, the sponson on the driver's side being empty. (Later 1972-73 cars had tanks on both sides.) In contrast to the star-shaped spoked wheels used on recent sports/racing and production Ferraris, the 312 PB had simple slotted alloy disc wheels, of 13-inch diameter in front and 15-inch in back.

When first tested in October 1970, the 312 PB had an aluminum body (this being quicker to construct and modify during testing, but giving way to fiberglass once the design was finalized). The aluminum-sheeted sponsons ended in the middle of the car below the radiators, with the curved lower edges of the tail leaving open spaces in front of the rear tires. Small vertical tabs or fences were applied to the front fenders. On the later fiberglass bodies the front fences were molded into the nose, the paneling of the side sponsons extended farther back, and the new fiberglass tail had slight fins with a low, full-width wing between them. For most of the car's early races a nose without headlights was used; for the 1971 Sebring 12-hour race and all of the 1972-73 events headlights were mounted.

For 1971 four 312 PB chassis were built and one car for Giunti/Merzario was sent to Buenos Aires in January for the opening round of the Manufacturers Championship. It more than lived up to expectations by qualifying for the front row, just four-hundredths of a second slower than the fastest Porsche 917. In the race it rushed away into a lead it held for five laps and Giunti was able to stay within 10 seconds of the Porsches until he ran into the back of a Matra that was being pushed along the track, irresponsibly and against the regulations, by its driver Jean-Pierre Beltoise. The Ferrari burst into flames and Giunti died of burns and head injuries. This tragic accident cost the Ferrari team one of its most promising drivers and damaged the car (0880) too severely to be raced again.

Of the other 312 PBs, the first two built (0876 and 0878) were used in most of the subsequent championship races (although only one 312 PB was entered in each race) while during 1971 0882 was apparently used only for testing. Giving Daytona a miss, the factory sent one 312 PB (0878) to Sebring for Ickx/Andretti, who put it on the front row again, this time next to the Penske 512 M of Mark Donohue/David Hobbs. The little Ferrari was the car best suited to Sebring and led for much of the race while the bigger cars made more frequent stops for fuel and brake pads, but the Formula 1-type transmission was not up to the job and failed in midrace when the 312 PB was running comfortably in the lead. But having gone nearly 700 miles, the transmission had lasted more than twice as long as required in its usual Formula 1 application.

The car won the pole for the Brands Hatch 1000-km race, handled by Ickx/Regazzoni. Ickx was leading when forced off the road by a spinning car and lost 10 minutes having minor damage repaired in the pits.

First 312 PB, essentially a Formula 1 boxer with two-seat bodywork, was first tested at Modena in October 1970; note tacked-on vanes.

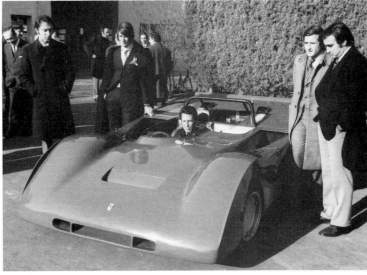

Drivers Nino Vaccarella, Arturo Merzario, Mario Andretti (in car), Ignazio Giunti and Clay Regazzoni at official debut of 312 PB in December; note lack of headlights.

Ronnie Peterson (who would drive for Ferrari the following year) inspects 312 PB at race debut in Buenos Aires in January 1971.

312 PB had headlights for 12-hour race at
Sebring, where Ickx (at wheel) and Andretti
led until the gearbox failed after 117 laps.

Ickx started from pole and led at Nurburgring
but 312 PB's engine overheated at mid-race.

Mechanics push 312 PB into truck at Watkins Glen; car worked up to first place in race but it was a starter motor that failed this time.

He and Regazzoni drove expertly to work the 312 PB up to second place but it was still three laps behind the winning Alfa Romeo 33 at the finish.

At Monza the flat-12 Ferrari once again started from the front row and once again had its chances spoiled by an accident. Ickx was first off the line at the drop of the flag but his race ended on the 13th lap when he hit the wreckage of a Porsche 907 that had crashed in front of him after it had touched fenders with a Ferrari 512 M. The rear of the 312 PB was badly damaged and the car was out of the race, but Ickx was unhurt.

The 312 PB could not match the lap times of the 5-liter cars on the high-speed Spa circuit and it was all Ickx could manage to hold on to third place behind the Gulf Porsches, despite his being the fastest driver on his home track. Regazzoni kept the car in third spot until crashing at approximately 180 mph when a slow car cut in front of him. Once more the car was badly damaged but its driver unhurt. After four crashes in five events, all caused by other cars being lapped, the Ferrari was overdue for some luck.

The team passed up the Targa Florio and sent the repaired car to the Nürburgring for the usual Ickx/Regazzoni pairing. Ickx, also a master of the Ring, had little trouble setting the fastest practice lap, a full nine seconds better than any other car. He gained a 40-second lead before handing over to Regazzoni at one-third distance. Regazzoni held on to the lead until mid-race when it was found that the overheating engine wouldn't hold water as a result of cracked cylinder heads, so the car was retired in the pits—at least it wasn't forced off the track this time!

For a car that had completed only one 1000-km race so far, 24 hours was too much to ask and Le Mans was left to the 5-liter machines. The next event was at the Österreichring, and the flat-12 Ferrari maintained form by starting from the front row, between two Porsches. Again driven by Ickx/Regazzoni, the 312 PB had revised suspension to suit new low-profile Firestone tires. The Ferrari took command of the race after the Porsches had early troubles and at three-quarter distance it was a lap ahead and increasing its margin when Regazzoni slid into a guardrail on a fast turn. This time no other driver was to blame; apparently the brakes had not been working properly, although the front of the car was too badly damaged for an examination to be made.

Andretti joined Ickx for the final 1971 championship race at Watkins Glen. The 312 PB was third fastest, starting from the second row for a change, but at least it was another Ferrari—the Donohue/Hobbs 512 M—that sat on the pole. The smaller Ferrari ran in fourth place during the first few laps, moved up to second when the Porsches had trouble, and found itself in the lead on lap 54 after the retirement of the 512 M. But this lead lasted just two laps; on a scheduled pit stop the starter motor would not function and the 312 PB was out.

The boxer Ferrari had performed consistently well all season, leading seven of its eight championship races and more than matching the speeds of the 5-liter cars, and just as consistently it had run into trouble—four serious crashes, one gearbox failure, one overheating engine, one starter failure and only one finish.

In contrast, the post-season Kyalami 9-hour race saw a repetition of Ferrari's 1970 victory with a 512 M. For the 1971 race two 312 PBs were sent, one of them a new car (0884) built to 1972 specifications with more compact bodywork fitting snugly around the low-profile tires, a wider cockpit opening as required by the next season's rules, and the twin, angled, vertical

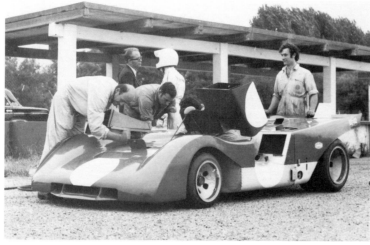

Modena circuit, September 1971: Peter Schetty (with Ing. Bussi) tests 312 PB. Water radiators are amidships, oil radiators above rear suspension, transmission oil cooler at back.

The following month Schetty tested 1972 version of 312 PB with wider cockpit opening required by rules. Car was second at Kyalami in November.

Peterson and Schenken won debut race at Buenos Aires in January 1972, beginning perfect record of twelve wins for twelve starts that season.

fins that had been seen on the earlier cars since the Monza race. The new car was about 2 inches lower than before but the space frame was built of heavier-gauge tubing to meet the new minimum-weight requirement of 650 kg (1430 pounds). The older car (0878), driven by Regazzoni and Brian Redman, had a trouble-free run (perhaps a reward for all the earlier misfortunes) to take first place. The new car, driven by Andretti/Ickx, led briefly but then had a 45-minute delay when it stopped out on the circuit, seemingly out of fuel but also plagued with battery trouble that made restarting difficult. After this the car was driven rapidly to a second-place finish, although 15 laps behind the Redman/Regazzoni 312 PB, and Andretti was credited with fastest lap.

Six additional cars were built for 1972, even numbers 0886 through 0896, in an all-out effort to restore Ferrari's sports car mastery. Peter Schetty, 1969 hillclimb champion with the boxer 212 E, was the team manager, taking four cars to each event, three to race and one as a spare. Another four remained at the factory for preparation, alternating so that usually no car would have to run two races in succession. Having had to repair the single entry after every race in 1971, the team was now going first class and it was obvious that the program had the Commendatore's full approval. The main drivers signed up for the season were Ferrari regulars Ickx, Regazzoni and Andretti, plus Redman, Ronnie Peterson and Tim Schenken, with Merzario to drive when Andretti's USAC commitments made him unavailable. In addition Sandro Munari, Helmut Marko and Carlos Pace were called on to drive the 312 PBs, the Italian rally expert to share a solo entry in the Targa Florio and the last two to share a fourth car at the Österreichring. This was a truly cosmopolitan line-up of great talent, comprising drivers of Belgian,

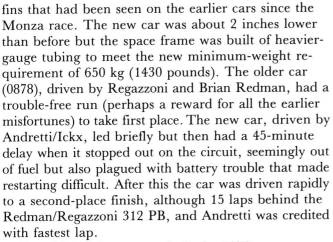

Redman gets out as Regazzoni prepares to take over fourth-place 312 PB at Daytona; note hose to right fuel tank, bottle for left.

Swiss, American, British, Swedish, Australian, Italian, Austrian and Brazilian nationality.

A Perfect Season

THE YEAR 1972 was a complete triumph for Ferrari, a lesson in total domination by a magnificent organization. The very light and maneuverable 312 PB now had approximately 445-450 bhp and the only serious contenders were Alfa Romeo, which never matched its 1971 form, and Mirage, which only began to challenge the Ferraris at the end of the year. Matra avoided a confrontation by reserving its efforts for Le Mans, which Ferrari in turn did not contest because the 312 PB was still considered unsuitable for the great distances involved in the 24-hour event. Thus the Ferrari-Matra battle did not occur until 1973.

The 1972 Buenos Aires 1000-km race was won by Ferrari newcomers Peterson/Schenken, with Regazzoni/Redman second. Ickx and Andretti had electrical and starter troubles, plus a puncture, but managed to finish tenth. They made up for that with a victory at Daytona (a 6-hour race that year), despite fuel injection problems; Peterson/Schenken were second and Regazzoni/Redman fourth.

In the Sebring and Brands Hatch events the same driver pairings were first and second. In the American 12-hour race the Regazzoni/Redman 312 PB broke a driveshaft while leading and the car caught fire as a result of a severed oil line; in the British 1000-km race their car managed to finish fifth despite losing oil.

At Brands Hatch the cars had appeared with additional panels below the upswept tails, so that the backs of the rear tires were covered. For Monza all-new, longer tails with low full-width wings were provided. This design, covering the back of the car as had the temporary panels at Brands Hatch, was used for the rest of the year with the wings set noticeably higher for the Watkins Glen event.

Ickx/Regazzoni won the rainy Monza 1000-km

127

This view of Schenken in second-place 312 PB
at Sebring shows open rear bodywork, enclosed
for later races in order to meet rules.

Peterson in the rain at Monza, where he set
fastest lap but was third behind a Porsche
908/3; note longer tail with full-width wing.

312 PB poses with 1949 166 MM Touring barchetta at opening festivities for Ferrari's Fiorano test track in April 1972.

Headlights on, 312 PBs of Ickx and Merzario run together at the Nurburgring; scoreboard shows that number 3 car of Peterson/Schenken, the ultimate winners, is ahead of them.

1973 version of 312 PB had longer wheelbase, improved aerodynamics including higher rear wing.

Redman and Merzario finished in car-number order at the Nurburgring. Number 2 car had oil radiator on side, lower rear deck with single air scoop.

race but the Peterson/Schenken Ferrari was beaten for second place by a Porsche 908/3 that had actually led when the track was flooded and visibility almost zero. Nearly every car left the track at one time or another, the Redman/Merzario 312 PB being too badly damaged in one of its excursions to continue the race. The winning average speed was only 106 mph, 40 mph slower than the year before.

By contrast, the Spa 1000-km race was a straightforward high-speed event, won by Redman/Merzario with Ickx/Regazzoni second. This time Schenken/Peterson were the unlucky pair; their car dropped out when the Swede was surprised by a damp section of track and crashed.

Alfa Romeo had been successful in the Targa Florio in the past and was looking forward to another win in 1972, as the Ferrari 312 PB was not thought to be tough enough for the long, rugged circuit. At the last minute Ferrari sent a single boxer for Munari, an excellent open-road driver, and Merzario. They did everything possible, winning the 492-mile race with a margin of only 16 seconds on the second place Alfa. This was an unexpected Ferrari victory against long odds; disappointing to Alfa Romeo, it kept the 312 PB's winning streak intact.

Scuderia Ferrari went back to its usual three-car line-up for the Nürburgring and scored another 1-2 victory. Peterson/Schenken were the victors with Redman/Merzario second. But for the first time that year the Ferraris were challenged in pure speed; one of the Mirages had the lead for awhile after Regazzoni crashed the third Ferrari trying to keep ahead of it.

The Österreichring race was unusual in that no Ferraris qualified for the front row, a Mirage and a Lola taking the first two positions. Ferrari had entered its spare car for Marko/Pace, so the red cars made up the next two rows. Every one of the 312 PBs encountered problems in the race, but these were minor compared to those of the opposition and Ferrari scored an almost unprecedented 1-2-3-4 sweep in the order Ickx/Redman, Marko/Pace, Peterson/Schenken and Merzario/Munari.

The last 1972 championship race was the Watkins Glen 6-hour event. Ferrari made it ten victories in ten starts with yet another 1-2 performance. Because the season was already a complete triumph for Maranello, the leading cars were allowed to duel at the finish and Ickx/Andretti beat Peterson/Schenken by just 14 seconds. The Merzario/Redman car retired with the only engine failure the team experienced all season.

During the series the 29 boxer entries scored 24 finishes. In only two races did Ferrari fail to back up the winner with a second place—at Monza because of the atrocious conditions that could even have cost Maranello a victory, and in the Targa Florio because no second Ferrari was entered. Ickx was the winner six times and every driver shared at least one victory, with the exception of Marko and Pace who were second in their only race for Ferrari.

Reduced Effort

AT THE END OF JULY Ferrari had shocked the racing world with another of his periodic retirement-from-racing announcements. In the past these had usually been in protest over FIA actions, but this time the complaint was the high cost of competition, certainly valid after the unlimited onslaught of 1972. If this was meant to draw further financial support from Fiat, it apparently worked, because the initial "no cars car for 1973" became "perhaps one car for Ickx" within a few weeks and finally an almost normal two-car team was announced for the 1973 championship. Ickx, Redman, Merzario and Pace were signed to drive, while Schenken and a new recruit, Carlos Reutemann, were lined up for an occasional third car, and the Sicilian Vaccarella drove in the Targa Florio.

At the end of 1972 the 312 PB of Merzario/Regazzoni won an easy victory in the Kyalami 9-hour race, Ferrari's third in a row in that event. This was Regazzoni's last Ferrari drive before moving to BRM for a season in Formula 1 and Alfa Romeo in Prototype races. Ickx set the fastest lap but the car he shared with Redman dropped out with valve failure. Both cars were 1973 versions with longer noses and the wheelbases lengthened to 2340 mm (92.1 inches) to improve stability. The bore and stroke were now 80.0 x 49.6 mm and the capacity 2991.8 cc, as on the latest Formula 1 boxer units; output was 450 bhp at 11,000 rpm. Goodyear tires were used for the first time (thus losing the services of Firestone-contracted Mario Andretti for 1973),

mounted on 13-inch wheels front and back.

The 1973 Manufacturers Championship was to be much more competitive than in 1972 and Ferrari had to work hard to keep up with its rivals, let alone ahead of them. In Group 5 (the Prototype category that had been called Group 6 in 1972) the French Matra team was contesting the entire series with its MS670 cars that had superb roadholding and V-12 engines that produced approximately 475 bhp compared to Ferrari's 450-460. The Mirages had only 440 bhp from their Ford Cosworth V-8s but were becoming more competitive race by race, while Alfa Romeo had a new flat-12 engine under development for its latest Tipo 33.

If these 3-liter rivals weren't enough, there was the threat of the Porsche Carreras in the Special Grand Touring class. These 2.7-liter Group 4 cars, the ancestors of the current, phenomenal 935 Turbos, were extremely fast and capable of winning the more arduous long-distance races, while a 3-liter Carrera version running as a Prototype in Group 5 was a threat for high placings in any of the races.

The Daytona race (back to its 24-hour duration) showed this clearly. Ferrari knew its 312 PB wasn't likely to last the distance and didn't enter, while Matra and Mirage could have saved themselves the trouble, all the fragile Group 5 cars retiring. A Porsche Carrera won and it was a 365 GTB/4 that scored crucial points for Ferrari by finishing second.

The Group 5 battle really began with the Vallelunga race and the Ferrari team was shocked to discover that not only was the 312 PB's power output less than the Matra's, but also the roadholding was

312 PBs had lengthened tails and revised noses with extra headlights for 1973 Le Mans 24-hour race; cars of Ickx/Redman (shown) and Schenken/Reutemann retired but Merzario/Pace took second.

inferior, the Ferrari having severe understeering problems. The Matras controlled the entire race, and even after their faster car dropped out the French team won, with the Reutemann/Schenken Ferrari second, a minute behind. Ickx/Redman were third (their 312 PB having Formula 1-type inboard rear brakes for the first time) and Pace/Merzario 4th. All three Ferraris had tall F1-type intakes, one for each side of the engine, and the output was now close to 460 bhp.

At Dijon, Matra repeated the performance, taking first and third places with the Ickx/Redman and Pace/Merzario Ferraris second and fourth. In an attempt to cure the understeer, Ferrari added full-width spoilers to the noses, but these forced the body down on the front tires, causing abnormal wear.

Though still ahead of Matra on points, Ferrari badly needed a victory at Monza to keep its championship hopes—and reputation—alive. Three Ferraris were entered for Ickx/Redman, Merzario/Pace and Schenken/Reutemann; these were unchanged except for a very unscientific solution to the understeering problem—the addition of 13 kg of lead to each nose! In fact, this worked well and the drivers reported improved handling. It was reliability that won the race for Ferrari, the Matras still being slightly faster, and Ickx/Redman and Schenken/Reutemann scored a popular 1-2 finish in the Italian race, with the one surviving Matra third. Merzario went out with gearbox failure on the seventh lap.

Mirage interrupted this two-way championship battle with a 1-2 victory of its own in the Spa race. Despite Ickx's expertise at Spa, which gave his 312 PB the pole position, the Matra was still the fastest car. But the Italian and French teams both experienced problems in mid-race and handed the lead to the now-reliable Mirages. The Ickx/Redman Ferrari stopped with a seized gearbox when in the lead and the Pace/Merzario car lost 5 minutes with a loose gearbox oil cooler when running second. It ended up fourth behind one of the Matras.

Alfa Romeo's flat-12 had made its debut at Spa and two of them joined the two Ferrari 312 PBs con-

testing the Targa Florio. A Porsche Carrera predictably won that race and became a championship contender on points, though it would continue to be an outsider on the high-speed circuits. In the Targa, the Merzario/Vaccarella Ferrari dropped out with another broken gearbox, strained by driving on a flat tire, and the Ickx/Redman car hit a rock and careened into a guardrail, so Ferrari scored no points in Sicily.

Ferrari outlasted the faster Matras at the Nürburgring, the two 312 PBs of Ickx/Redman and Merzario/Pace coming in 1-2 after the French cars had engine failures. The new Alfa Romeos were also fast (Ickx could not match the times of either Francois Cevert's Matra or Rolf Stommelen's Alfa 33 TT12, although the timekeepers erroneously put him ahead of the latter on the starting grid) but both of them retired early in the race. The Merzario/Pace car had several modifications intended to improve the airflow to the rear wing: The main oil cooler was moved from above the engine to a position just ahead of the right rear wheel and fed by a scoop below the right-hand water radiator, while the two fuel-injection air intakes were replaced by a single taller one in the center. However, this car did not seem to handle any better than the usual type.

With the outcome of the season still much in doubt (even though Ferrari had 95 points after the Nürburgring, a lead of 31 over Matra), Maranello had to reconsider the 312 PB's chances in the Le Mans 24-hour race. Even if the Ferraris had only a slight chance of lasting the distance, Matra (which had won in 1972) could not be allowed to run unopposed. Eleven days before Le Mans a 312 PB ran a successful 17-hour trouble-free test at Monza and the three-car Ferrari entry was confirmed.

Matra won the race for the second year in a row, but the Ferrari challenge was strong. Each of the three 312 PBs had held the lead (Ferrari being in front of Matra for 15 of the first 17 hours) and the Ickx/Redman car was only a lap behind after 23 hours when it dropped out. The Reutemann/Schenken 312 PB had failed at 11 hours but the Mer-

Extensively revised 312 PB for 1974 was never raced. Aerodynamics were probably no more effective than they were attractive, and Niki Lauda was only interested in Formula 1. Compare car with extremely simple early versions of PB.

Writer shoots from cockpit as Harley Cluxton's 312 PBs run around Scottsdale airport.

zario/Pace car lasted the full 24 hours and finished second, keeping Maranello ahead of the French team on points, 110 to 84. The Le Mans 312 PBs had run with longer tails, the rear decks sweeping downward under the wings, plus extra pairs of lights mounted in front under flush plastic panels.

One of the two cars entered for the Österreichring 1000-km practiced with the long tail but ran with the regular type; the other car had the side oil-cooler layout first tried at the Nürburgring. A longer-wheelbase version had been tested but was not ready for the Austrian event. In the race, Matra made Ferrari's championship position more precarious with a 1-2 victory; the Ickx/Redman 312 PB was third and the Pace/Merzario car sixth behind two Mirages. This result narrowed the margin to 18 points (122-104) and the outcome now depended on the

Watkins Glen 6-hour race in mid-July.

Matra took the title in America with a third successive victory. The Ickx/Redman and Pace/Merzario 312 PBs were second and third in the event, and the former car's finish raised Ferrari's point total to 127, compared to 124 for Matra. But the cancellation of the final race at Buenos Aires meant that Ferrari could only count its seven best performances out of the ten events actually held, and Matra ended up on top, 124-115. This technicality was certainly just in its effect, because Matra had won five races to Ferrari's two (Porsche had also won two, and Mirage one). The Ferrari clearly lacked development in 1973, and the absence of Peter Schetty meant that team management also fell below the magnificent 1972 standards. In fairness, it must be emphasized that the opposition was much stronger than the previous year, and none of Ferrari's rivals was also involved in Formula 1.

During the winter of 1973-74 Ferrari continued to test further versions of the 312 PB with heavily modified bodywork, particularly at the rear where the airscoop/wing arrangement was complex to say the least. Regazzoni was back at Ferrari for 1974, along with a new recruit, Niki Lauda. The Austrian had little interest in the sports/racing category, wishing to concentrate on Formula 1, and the results in the latter area since 1974 have justified Ferrari's decision to abandon the sports/racing category. There have been no official Ferrari entries in international sports car races since 1973, so the 312 PB was the last, and in 1972 form certainly the greatest, Ferrari of this type.

In the Fall of 1978 the author had the opportunity to experience the performance of the 312 PB through a generous invitation extended by Harley Cluxton of Grand Touring Cars, Inc. of Scottsdale, Arizona. Cluxton owned three of the potent 312 PBs at that time, serial numbers 0886, 0890 and 0894. These were basically similar but differed in various details, such as wheelbase, rear wheel size, rear brake location, oil cooler mounting, air scoops, rear wing, etc. Cluxton was able to use the access roads of the Scottsdale airport as his own race track, and the author was a passenger on high-speed runs which demonstrated the cars' phenomenal acceleration, braking and handling, of a level which cannot be compared to any road car, even a Ferrari. The engine note was loud enough to hurt the ears but the unit proved remarkably tractable. As prepared by Cluxton's crew, the 312 PBs would fire up at a moment's notice and gave the impression that they would run all day without a fuss. On the other hand, the track performance was exhilarating; as the passenger seat was not really big enough for normal use, the author was forced to brace himself in a position that put his head well into the airstream and also gave his legs the full effect of deceleration on braking. This kind of experience makes one regret Ferrari's abandonment of sports car racing.

Chapter 11

365 GT/BB Boxer for the Road

WAS IT INEVITABLE that the Formula 1, hillclimb and long-distance sports/racing boxers would be followed by a flat-12 Ferrari Gran Turismo car? According to the Maranello scheme of things, the incorporation of exotic racing technology in the customers' road cars is almost a foregone conclusion. And by late 1971, although only in its third year of production, Ferrari's top-of-the-line GT car, the 365 GTB/4 Daytona was beginning to look like a classic: beautiful, fast, but with a front-engine chassis that fell short of even early-Seventies standards of handling and maneuverability.

Even so, the appearance of the prototype Berlinetta Boxer at the Turin show in November was a surprise. The sleek, Pininfarina-styled 2-seater, Ferrari's first mid-engine 12-cylinder production machine, looked much as expected—in effect, a scaled-up Dino 246 GT, though less rounded, with lines tightly drawn around the more potent package. The low, nearly flat nose contained the water radiator and the retractable headlights, while a lower set of driving lights could be converted electromagnetically into fog lamps by diffracting strips that changed the focus. A barely suggested fender line curved over the large wheel arches, but the body form was strongly divided by a horizontal line around the car with matte black paint below. The bodywork was steel, with hood, doors and rear deck of aluminum. A racing-type parallelogram wiper kept the large, steeply raked windshield well swept. The inset rear window had a small wing behind it, this not only adding to the car's stability at high speed but also helping the flow of air to the carburetor intakes on the rear deck.

The real surprise was the engine. It *was* a boxer, and not just a detuned version of the 3-liter 312 B unit which had two years of Formula 1 and one season of sports/racing competition behind it. The BB's engine was a big 4.4 liters, with the same 81 x 71-mm bore and stroke dimensions of the Daytona but differing in every other way. As displayed at Turin, the engine's air cleaners were removed so that the four beautiful Weber 40 IF3C triple-throat downdraft carburetors could be admired. The power output of the 4390-cc flat-12 was then given as 360 bhp DIN at 7500 rpm (the Daytona's V-12 gave 352 bhp at the same engine speed); on the early production Boxers, designated 365 GT/BB, no less than 380 bhp was quoted at 7200 rpm, with a compression ratio of 8.8:1.

By this time, all Ferraris had four overhead camshafts, but the BB had only two valves per cylinder, 24 in all, compared to the 48 of the smaller but

Pininfarina design sketch for Berlinetta Boxer.

higher-revving and more highly stressed 312 B. The cylinder heads and block were of aluminum alloy and the crankshaft ran in seven main bearings. The most novel feature of the power unit was the position of the 5-speed transmission, *under* the back of the engine rather than behind. With a wet sump, the 365 BB engine had a higher crankshaft line than the racing units, so Ferrari's engineers decided to reduce the length of the wheelbase by running a shaft (driven by a set of step-down gears) back under the engine, with the gearbox ahead of the final drive. The drive train was offset to the left, to allow room for the engine sump on the right, and the rear axle line was below the number nine and ten cylinders.

Although saving about 200 mm (roughly 8 inches) in length with this layout, the Berlinetta Boxer still had a wheelbase of 2500 mm (98.4 inches), 100 mm longer than Ferrari's almost standard dimension of 2400 on previous front-engine GT Berlinettas. Front and rear track were 1500 and 1520 mm respectively; the length was 4360 mm (171.6 inches), the width 1800 mm and the height only 1120 mm. The original weight of 1120 kg quoted for the Turin show car was optimistic in the extreme; Ferrari persisted with this figure in its literature on the production BBs, but a U.S. version tested by *Road & Track* magazine weighed 3420 pounds, and it is unlikely that any road Boxer weighed less than 3000.

Replacement for the Daytona

THE DAYTONA CONTINUED in production throughout 1972, being supplanted by the BB in the Spring of 1973. As was the regular procedure for Ferrari Berlinettas, the Pininfarina-designed bodywork was produced by Scaglietti, effectively the factory's own *carrozzeria*. Previous high-performance Ferraris were quick to come to the United States, but examples of the BB were rare initially because of the extremely

*365 GT/BB prototype photographed at Pininfarina
studio in 1971. Most details remained on production car.*

Wind-tunnel test at Pininfarina Galleria del Vento.

Engine and interior views of first production BB.

complex Federal requirements for safety and exhaust emissions, which the factory was unwilling to meet on a production basis. Ferrari cannot be criticized for this, as the number of cars involved was so low that the engineering effort would have been astronomical on a per-car basis. The result was that cars had to be brought to the U.S. individually, with the owner posting a bond and being responsible for making the car conform with Federal standards. The different ways in which this was done (or not really done!) meant cars of widely varying output and performance.

Road & Track's 365 GT/BB was tested in June of 1975. Its output was figured at 344 bhp net at 7200 rpm, and at the 3420-lb curb weight already mentioned, it was not as fast in acceleration as the editors hoped, taking 7.2 seconds to reach 60 mph, 14.8 to 100 and 15.5 to the quarter-mile. On the other hand, the top speed of 175 reached in 5th made this Boxer the fastest road car R&T had ever tested up to that time, and the handling was found to be excellent, with a moderate built-in understeer which could be turned into power-on oversteer in tight corners. The lateral acceleration on the 100-foot radius skidpad was an impressive 0.845 g. Without the front air dam later built into the 512 BB, the 365 GT/BB became a bit light at the front end at speeds over 120 mph, with a consequent demand for full attention to the steering.

At the same time that the author visited Harley Cluxton and rode in his 312 PB sports/racing cars (Chapter 10), he had the opportunity to drive a 365 GT/BB and ventured close to 150 mph (around 240 km/h on the speedometer, probably somewhat

4.4-liter BB engine was completely different from 3-liter racing boxers, with crankcase above transmission. Output was 360 bhp DIN.

optimistic) on a straight stretch near Scottsdale. At all times the car felt stable and controllable, perhaps so much so that the actual rate of travel seemed deceptively slow, even a little less exciting than one would expect. Acceleration was not phenomenal, though satisfying, and it was obvious that the purpose of the car was sophisticated high-speed cruising, with a chassis good enough to maintain speed through a variety of road conditions. The BB was not as maneuverable or as fun to drive as a 308 GTB or GTS, which cars are quite frankly better suited to American conditions. While driving around the perimeter of the Scottsdale airport (Cluxton's test track for his Le Mans cars and other exotics), the author experienced the power oversteer reported by *Road & Track*, but the steering was precise enough to allow a face-saving recovery.

In November 1976 *Car and Driver* magazine tested a legalized 365 GT/BB, prepared by Luigi Chinetti's expert designer, Dick Fritz. In addition to the engine changes to make it emissions-legal (revised valve timing and twin air pumps, with catalytic packs on the exhaust pipes), this car had redesigned, larger bumpers to make it crash-legal, all the modifications adding approximately $14,000 to the $38,000 base price for a total of over $52,000. But, as we will see in Chapter 12, this was nothing compared to the cost of a U.S.-legal BB 512. Fritz's modifications to the 365 GT/BB left it with a respectable 340 bhp and a curb weight of 3498 pounds. It was more responsive than the example tested by *Road & Track*, accelerating to 60 mph in 6.1 seconds, to 100 in 14.1 and to the quarter-mile in 14.4. Fritz's Amerispec operation, in Danbury, Connecticut, was one of at least

four outfits specializing in the legalizing of Ferraris; the others have been ACI of Harbor City, California, ACC of Spring Valley, New York and the Alpine Road of San Jose, California.

A normal European version of the 365 GT/BB (but with right-hand drive) was tested by *Motor* magazine in England in October 1975. The factory figure of 380 bhp DIN was quoted for this car, but no dimension or weights were given. Acceleration to 60 mph was done in 6.5 seconds, between the figures recorded by the two American magazines, but the car was quicker at the top end, reaching 100 mph in 13.5. On the roads available no maximum speed run was made, but 135 mph was achieved in 4th. The price was given as £17,487, close to $40,000 at the 1975 exchange rate. The official Italian price at the factory was initally L.18,290,000 in 1973, increasing to 24,375,000 by 1976; this was equivalent to about $30-33,000.

Shown at Turin in 1974, Pininfarina's Studio Cr 25 was an aerodynamic coupe carrying Ferrari identification and ostensibly designed around a front-mounted 365 Boxer engine. The engine was never actually mounted in the car but wind-tunnel tests gave a Cx = 0.256, hence its designation.

Minimal BB Competition

THE 365 GTB/4 DAYTONA had a long and successful competition history, but the factory made no real effort to make the 365 GT/BB competitive in racing. The car was heavy, the rival Porsches were already extremely highly developed for Group 5 racing, and Scuderia Ferrari had found that its successes in For-

Ostensibly designed around a BB engine to be mounted in front, Studio Cr 25 was 1974 show car built by Pininfarina as aerodynamic project. Lacking an engine, it couldn't have beaten camels.

Two 365 GT/BB engines in the Maranello plant, where final assembly took place.

Frames and bodywork for Berlinetta Boxers were built by Carrozzeria Scaglietti in Modena.

NART BB was sixth in 1975 Sebring 12-hour race. With 5-liter engine, original NART BB was again placed sixteenth at Le Mans in 1978 event. Rear fenders are extended on this much-modified car.

mula 1 could only be extended by a total commitment to Grand Prix racing. As a result, there was never a factory racing version of the 365 GT/BB, although the North American Racing Team example, the only one to compete with any regularity, probably had the benefit of minimal factory advice. The NART car was lightened to some degree by the removal of non-essential equipment, it had wider bodywork to accommodate the larger Goodyear racing tires, and it is likely that the engine output was 400-420 bhp. But it was never especially competitive. In 1975 it retired after one lap at Daytona, finished 6th at Sebring, broke down in practice and did not race at Road Atlanta, and retired after the engine caught fire at Lime Rock.

In 1976 the NART Boxer did not race but it was extensively modified for the 1977 Le Mans 24-hour event. Driven by Francois Migault and Lucien Guitteny, it finished 16th after being delayed for two hours to replace a flywheel gasket. The same two drivers ran the car at Daytona in 1978, running as high as 8th but dropping to 22nd at the finish after experiencing electrical trouble.

In contrast to the 365 GT/BB, the 512 version of the Berlinetta Boxer has received more extensive competition development, including a highly modified factory racing version, as discussed in Chapter 12.

In the Summer of 1976 the first details of the 5-liter BB 512 were announced, the larger-engined car supplanting the 365 GT/BB on the Maranello production lines early in 1977. As Ferrari's first production mid-engine twelve, the 365 GT/BB brought state-of-the-art technology to the firm's road cars. It was challenged in pure performance by the Porsche Turbo and the Lamborghini Countach, but for all-around high-speed transportation it was certainly the ultimate, this distinction now being enjoyed by its successor, the BB 512.

Chapter 12

BB 512 **Five-Liter Exotic**

WHILE SCUDERIA FERRARI'S concentration on Formula 1 meant that little valuable facilities or personnel could be "wasted" on GT racing, the prestige of having the ultimate road car was still important to the Maranello engineers, and certainly to Enzo Ferrari himself. The challenge of Lamborghini's Countach, in maximum speed if not in overall refinement, called for a reply from Ferrari. During 1975-76 a 5-liter version of the Berlinetta Boxer was developed; designated the BB 512 (for 5-liter, 12-cylinder, instead of the single-cylinder capacity being given), it did not have the great increase in power output or top speed expected, Ferrari choosing (wisely it would seem) to improve the torque, drivability and overall sophistication of the machine. The bore and stroke became 82 x 78 mm, with a total displacement of 4942 cc. The compression ratio was raised to 9.2:1, but the output was quoted at a relatively modest 360 bhp, albeit at a lower engine speed of 6800 rpm. The torque became 44 kg/m (343 lb/ft) at 4600 rpm.

The wheelbase and front track remained the same but the rear track was increased to 61.5 inches and wider 9-inch wheels were mounted at the back. There were several exterior changes, including an air dam below the nose, NACA-type intakes in the rocker panels ahead of the rear wheels, revised taillights and more extensive louvering in the top of the engine cover.

If the relatively conservative changes did not result in quite the supercar that *some* Ferrari enthusiasts had hoped for, the maximum speed was marginally increased to 188 mph and the overall performance was more usable. With Boxers imported into America having to be converted independently, there being no factory-built U.S.-legal version, there is naturally a wide variation in the performance of individual BB 512s on this side of the Atlantic. *Road & Track* magazine tested a well-prepared example in its March 1978 issue; weighing 3615 pounds (compared to the figure of 3340 quoted in the factory instruction book for the European version), it reached the quarter-mile in a quick 14.2 seconds and was considered capable of achieving the 188-mph maximum even though sufficient road was not available during the test. Most important, the BB 512 was found to be a totally successful automobile, with the reliability and attention to comfort and detail lacking in most other exotic cars. Living with a Berlinetta Boxer could be a relatively normal proposition compared to the demands of maintaining a Countach.

The 365 GT/BB had received little or no factory racing development, but the BB 512 competed on a more serious level, with no less than five cars running at Le Mans in 1978 and a Silhouette version appearing in 1979. In the 1978 French race there were four BB 512s (two French, one Belgian and one American entry), all with modified noses, Formula 1-type (front) wings mounted at the back, and fairly mild fender flares to cover the wider-than-standard Michelin tires. These revisions were tested at Fiorano earlier in the year. The most interesting feature visually was the extended nose seen on the Chinetti entry and one of the two Pozzi machines; this design had flush driving lights flanking an oval air entry reminiscent of the 250 GTOs and 330 LMBs raced 15 years earlier. The fifth BB at the 1978 Le Mans race was the only one to finish. This was the old NART-built 365 GT/BB, now fitted with a 5-liter engine but still having the fatter bodywork and Goodyear tires. Again the pairing of Migault/Guitteny brought the Boxer into 16th place; the retirements of the newer BB 512s were blamed on transmission failures.

Silhouette BBs

THE FIRST BERLINETTA BOXERS to show real factory racing input were the three Silhouette BB 512s run at Daytona in 1979. These were extensively reworked beneath their all-new, Pininfarina wind-tunnel-tested bodywork, and had the benefit of some track testing

First BB 512 leaving Maranello factory for road test early in 1976. External differences were front air dam and NACA scoops on sides of body.

Overhead view of BB 512, from Ferrari brochure, shows car completely opened up.

BB 512 cockpit, from same brochure. Speedometer goes to 330 km/h (equivalent to 205
mph); tachometer redlines at 7000 rpm.

John Dinkel drags U.S.-legal BB 512 at Orange
County Raceway for 1978 Road & Track test.

BB 512 under construction at new body
plant at Maranello in September 1978.

Berlinetta Boxers converted in U.S. had bigger
bumpers in addition to required engine modifications.

Pozzi BB 512 for 1978 Le Mans was tested at Fiorano in May with F1-type front wing at back.

Yellow Belgian BB 512 for Beurlys/Pilette in 1978 Le Mans race had unusual front dam.

Pozzi BBs had two different noses at Le Mans; number 88 was fairly standard while 89 had extension with oval intake resembling 250 GTO.

Turbocharged BB 512 prepared by Jean-Louis Chateau for 1977 Le Mans did not run. Called 512 Turbo GTP, it produced about 520 bhp.

Three BB 512 Silhouettes ran at Daytona in 1979; two Pozzi machines were withdrawn after crash of NART car with tire failure on banking.

*Known as BB 512 LMs, four Silhouette cars
(one Beurlys, two Pozzi and one NART) ran in
the 1979 Le Mans 24-hour race; only the
yellow number 61 Beurlys car finished, twelfth.*

at the Fiorano circuit that winter, including laps by the new Formula 1 team driver Jody Scheckter. But it became apparent that this preparation was in fact minimal, the one NART and two Pozzi cars not being set up properly with the Michelins supplied to take the heavy demands of the banked Daytona track. A tire failure caused the NART machine to crash and the decision was made to withdraw the two French-entered BBs before an even worse accident might occur. The most notable result of the 1979 Daytona race was the second-place finish of the old front-engine 365 GTB/4 Daytona of Adamowicz/ Morton, who might even have won if the leading Porsche, already in trouble, had encountered a few more problems.

The Silhouette BB 512s were approximately 16

inches longer than standard, with smooth fender fairings and the roof line extended all the way back to the tail, which had a wing mounted between two vertical fins. Ten-inch-wide wheels were mounted in front and thirteens at the back, the transmission had its own oil radiator and the weight was 1070-1080 kg (2359-2381 pounds) as actually checked at Daytona. Equipped with fuel injection, the engine produced 480 bhp at 7200 rpm.

Although they were withdrawn, the performance of the Silhouette BBs at Daytona (the Ballot-Lena/Le-clére car qualified thirteenth fastest at 1:57.32) suggested a good chance for high placings if not overall victory at Le Mans. However, the cars were not really fast on the French circuit, none of the four entries breaking the four-minute barrier in practice. In the

*No less than six cars, four BB 512 LM/80
and two LM/79, ran at Le Mans in 1980;
tenth-place finish of Pozzi number 76 was
the best ever for a BB in the French event.*

race the one NART and two Pozzi BB 512s failed to
finish; the latter two machines crashed avoiding slower
cars and this was particularly unfortunate in the case
of the Andruet/Dini car which was running a good
sixth at the time (19 hours) and might well have
ended up fourth overall. The sole Boxer to finish was
the Belgian entry driven by Beurlys/Faure/O'Rourke/
De Dryver into twelfth position after many troubles.

In 1980 the Silhouette BB 512s ran again at
Daytona (a single Chinetti car) and Le Mans (no less
than six cars: three entries from Pozzi, one from
Chinetti, one from Rosso in England and one from
Bellancauto in Italy). In neither of the 24-hour races
were they threats for the Porsches or the sports prototypes, but at Le Mans there was at least a notable improvement in performance, including a 3:58.4 lap in

practice by the Ballot-Lena/Andruet/Dieudonné car (a
Pozzi entry) and a tenth-place finish, the best ever for
a BB at Le Mans, by another Pozzi machine driven
by Dieudonné/Xhenceval/Regout. All three of the
French-entered Berlinetta Boxers had an unusual co-
sponsorship from European University of Antwerp;
several business administration students dreamed up
the scheme wherein the University provided the
finance while they sold promotional items, enjoyed the
race and wrote a thesis on the experience!

While still far from its ultimate potential as a racing
car, the Silhouette BB 512 has shown slow, if steady,
progress. No turbocharged BBs have been raced so
far, but there was an interesting one-off example built
privately to the order of an unnamed Hong Kong en-
trant for the 1977 Le Mans race. Prepared by Jean-

145

Paul Pappalardo's BB 512 LM/80 (32131).

*With 935-type body panels, AIR Berlinetta Boxer
(serial 17577) prepared for 1981 IMSA racing
looked more like Porsche than Ferrari.*

*Turbocharged spyder conversion of BB 512
was made by Al Mardikian of Trend Imports.*

Louis Château, who had previous experience turbo-charging Porsches, the car was not satisfactory and the owner decided not to race it. Château expected about 520 bhp to be available in the long-distance version of the turbo engine but did not find the boxer's lubrication system sufficient for a proper racing conversion. In addition to the engine development, the turbo Boxer had extensive modifications to its bodywork, including a nose somewhat reminiscent of the Porsche 917 and a short, high tail with an almost full-width wing. This car was called the 512 Turbo GTP although it was not, of course, an official factory designation.

An American-built one-off turbocharged BB 512, strictly a road car, was produced by Al Mardikian of Trend Imports (a Hermosa Beach, California shop specializing in the legalizing of Boxers). Converted into Targa-style spyder bodywork as well, it was tested briefly by *Road Test* magazine and found to be capable of under-five-second 0-60 mph times and a best quarter-mile run of 11.7 seconds/111 mph. The price for the fully converted car was computed at $130,000.

If the racing potential of the Berlinetta Boxer has been deceptive and so far disappointing, the design remains the one true super-high-performance machine for regular road use, and as such keeps Ferrari's reputation at the very top of the enthusiast's category. The tradition of constantly developing better road machinery from the expertise gained in racing is still the guiding influence at Maranello. But as the factory entered the 1980s it was clear that the racing and production programs were really separate and distinct; both were justified as promoting the Italian high-performance car image in general and that of the parent Fiat organization in particular. Before 1980 it had seemed unlikely that we would see road Ferraris as race winners in the near future, but a revision of the GT racing rules to come closer to production-based equipment, something Ferrari would like to see, could allow that. The world standards for safety, drivability and fuel economy require a sophisticated compromise, even for an exotic car, and Ferrari has an entirely revised BB under development for 1982. The demands of racing have become ever more specialized and for a BB to win, say, Le Mans, is still not highly probable. But by winning World Championships in Formula 1 throughout the 1970s and producing BBs for the discriminating owner, Ferrari's boxer technology has led the way in both fields.

We may even see a front-engine Ferrari boxer, if Pininfarina's Pinin show car—a four-door sedan, no less—should be the prototype for a production car. Basically a styling study to celebrate the *carrozzeria's* fiftieth anniversary, the Pinin nevertheless had a BB 512 power plant under its hood. This engine may not have actually driven the Pinin's wheels on a road, but Ferrari works fast when he decides to do something and there may one day be a Berlina Boxer.

One-off BB 512 convertible built by Chinetti in 1981.

Pinin, the first Ferrari four-door Berlina, was produced by Pininfarina in 1980 as design study with BB 512 engine in front.

CHASSIS	NO.	DRIVER(S)	PRACTICE TIME (QUAL. POS.)	RESULT

512 F1

Watkins Glen (USA), 4 October 1964

| 512 F1 | 8 | Bandini | 1:13.83 (8) | R, 57 laps, engine |

Mexico City (MEX), 25 October 1964

| 512 F1 | 8 | Bandini | 1:58.60 (3) | 3rd, 65 laps |

East London (ZA), 1 January 1965

| 512 F1 | 2 | Bandini | 1:29.3 (6) | 15th, 66 laps, not running at finish |

Siracusa (I), 4 April 1965 (non-championship)

| 512 F1 | 22 | Bandini | 1:47.6 (5) | 3rd, 56 laps |

Silverstone (GB), 15 May 1965 (non-championship)

| 512 F1 | 2 | Bandini | 1:32.3 (4) | 7th, 51 laps |

Monte Carlo (MC), 30 May 1965

| 512 F1 | 17 | Bandini | 1:33.0 (4) | 2nd, 100 laps |

Spa-Francorchamps (B), 13 June 1965

| 512 F1 | 2 | Bandini | 3:54.0 (15) | 9th, 30 laps |

Clermont-Ferrand (F), 27 June 1965

| 512 F1 | 4 | Bandini | 3:19.1 (3) | R, 37 laps, accident |

Silverstone (GB), 10 July 1965

| 512 F1 | 1 | Surtees | 1:31.3 (5) | 3rd, 80 laps |

Zandvoort (NL), 18 July 1965

| 512 F1 | 2 | Surtees | 1:31.0 (4) | 7th, 79 laps |

Nürburgring (D), 1 August 1965

| 512 F1 | 7 | Surtees | 8:27.8 (4) | R, 11 laps, gear selector |

Monza (I), 12 September 1965

| 512 F1 | 4 | Bandini | 1:37.2 (5) | 4th, 76 laps |
| 512 F1 | 8 | Surtees | 1:36.1 (2) | R, 35 laps, clutch |

Watkins Glen (USA), 3 October 1965

| 512 F1 | 2 | Bandini | 1:11.73 (5) | 4th, 109 laps |
| 512 F1 | 14 | Rodriguez | 1:13.00 (15) | 5th, 109 laps |

Mexico City (MEX), 24 October 1965

| 512 F1 | 2 | Bandini | 1:57.31 (7) | 8th, 62 laps |
| 512 F1 | 14 | Rodriguez | 1:59.06 (14) | 7th, 62 laps |

212 E Montagna

Ampus (F), 30 March 1969 (non-championship)

| 212 E 0862 | — | Schetty | — | 1st, 3:56.70, record |

Volterra (I), 11 May 1969 (non-championship)

| 212 E 0862 | — | Schetty | — | 1st, 5:12.60, record |

CHASSIS	NO.	DRIVER(S)	PRACTICE TIME (QUAL. POS.)	RESULT
Montseny (E), 25 May 1969				
212 E 0862	—	Schetty	—	1st, 9:12.46, record
Rossfeld (D), 8 June 1969				
212 E 0862	104	Schetty	—	1st, 6:27.91
Mont Ventoux (F), 22 June 1969				
212 E 0862	131	Schetty	—	1st, 10:00.50, record
Trento-Bondone (I), 13 July 1969				
212 E 0862	197	Schetty	—	1st, 10:58.61, record
Freiburg-Schauinsland (D), 27 July 1969				
212 E 0862	88	Schetty	—	1st, 10:48.03 (two runs); 5:22.16, record
Cesana-Sestriere (I), 3 August 1969				
212 E 0862	380	Schetty	—	1st, 4:53.30, record
Ollon-Villars (CH), 31 August 1969				
212 E 0862	181	Schetty	—	1st, 7:37.32 (two runs); 3:47.54, record

312 B / 312 B2 / 312 B3 / 312 T / 312 T2 / 312 T3 / 312 T4 / 312 T5 F1

CHASSIS	NO.	DRIVER(S)	PRACTICE TIME (QUAL. POS.)	RESULT
Kyalami (ZA), 7 March 1970				
312 B 001	17	Ickx	1:20.0 (5)	R, 59 laps, engine
Jarama (E), 19 April 1970				
312 B 001	2T	Ickx	—	—
312 B 002	2	Ickx	1:24.7 (7)	R, 0 laps, accident
Monte Carlo (MC), 10 May 1970				
312 B 001	26	Ickx	1:25.5 (5)	R, 11 laps, driveshaft
312 B 003	26T	Ickx	—	—
Spa-Francorchamps (B), 7 June 1970				
312 B 001	27T	Ickx	—	—
312 B 002*	28	Giunti	3:32.4 (8)	4th, 28 laps
312 B 003	27	Ickx	3:30.7 (4)	8th, 26 laps
*New chassis				
Zandvoort (NL), 21 June 1970				
312 B 001	25	Ickx	1:18.93 (3)	3rd, 79 laps; fastest lap, 1:19.23
312 B 002	26T	Regazzoni	—	—
312 B 003	25T	Ickx	—	—
"	26	Regazzoni	1:19.48 (6)	4th, 79 laps
Clermont-Ferrand (F), 5 July 1970				
312 B 001	10T	Ickx	—	—
312 B 002	11	Giunti	3:01.85 (11)	14th, 35 laps
312 B 003	10	Ickx	2:58.22 (1)	R, 16 laps, valve
Brands Hatch (GB), 19 July 1970				
312 B 001	3T	Ickx	—	—
312 B 002	4	Regazzoni	1:25.8 (6)	4th, 80 laps
312 B 003	3	Ickx	1:25.1 (3)	R, 6 laps, differential
Hockenheim (D), 2 August 1970				
312 B 001	10T	Ickx	—	—
"	15	Regazzoni	1:59.8 (3)	R, 30 laps, spin
312 B 002	15T	Regazzoni	—	—
312 B 003	10	Ickx	1:59.5 (1)	2nd, 50 laps; fastest lap, 2:00.5

CHASSIS	NO.	DRIVER(S)	PRACTICE TIME (QUAL. POS.)	RESULT
Österreichring (A), 16 August 1970				
312 B 001	12	Ickx	1:39.86 (3)	1st, 60 laps; fastest lap, 1:40.4 (tie)
312 B 002	14	Giunti	1:40.21 (5)	7th, 59 laps
312 B 003	27	Regazzoni	1:39.70 (2)	2nd, 60 laps; fastest lap, 1:40.4 (tie)
Monza (I), 6 September 1970				
312 B 001	2T	Ickx	1:24.37	—
312 B 002	6	Giunti	1:24.74 (5)	R, 14 laps, fuel meter
312 B 003	2	Ickx	1:24.10 (1)	R, 25 laps, transmission
312 B 004	4	Regazzoni	1:24.39 (3)	1st, 68 laps; fastest lap, 1:25.2
St. Jovite (CDN), 20 September 1970				
312 B 001	18	Ickx	1:31.6 (2)	1st, 90 laps
312 B 004	19	Regazzoni	1:31.9 (3)	2nd, 90 laps; fastest lap, 1:32.2
Watkins Glen (USA), 4 October 1970				
312 B 001	3	Ickx	1:03.07 (1)	4th, 107 laps; fastest lap, 1:02.74
312 B 004	4	Regazzoni	1:04.30 (6)	13th, 101 laps
Mexico City (MEX), 25 October 1970				
312 B 001	3	Ickx	1:42.41 (3)	1st, 65 laps; fastest lap, 1:43.11
312 B 004	4	Regazzoni	1:41.86 (1)	2nd, 65 laps
Kyalami (ZA), 6 March 1971				
312 B 001	4	Ickx	1:19.2 (8)	8th, 78 laps
312 B 002	6	Andretti	1:19.0 (4)	1st, 79 laps; fastest lap, 1:20.3
312 B 004	5	Regazzoni	1:18.7 (3)	3rd, 79 laps
312 B2 005	5T	Regazzoni	—	—
Brands Hatch (GB), 21 March 1971 (non-championship)				
312 B2 005	5	Regazzoni	1:26.0 (3)	1st, 50 laps
Ontario (USA), 28 March 1971 (non-championship, two heats)				
312 B 001	4	Ickx	1:41.531 (3)	5th / R = 11th, 34 laps
312 B 002	5	Andretti	1:43.542 (12)	1st / 1st = 1st, 64 laps
Barcelona (E), 18 April 1971				
312 B 002	6	Andretti	1:26.9 (8)	R, 50 laps, fuel pump
312 B 003	4	Ickx	1:25.9 (1)	2nd, 75 laps; fastest lap, 1:25.1
312 B 004	5	Regazzoni	1:26.0 (2)	R, 13 laps, engine
312 B2 005	5T	Regazzoni	1:30.6	—
Monte Carlo (MC), 23 May 1971				
312 B 002	6	Andretti	1:43.4	—
312 B 003	4T	Ickx	—	—
"	6T	Andretti	1:40.0	Non-starter, did not qualify
312 B2 005	5	Regazzoni	1:26.1 (11)	R, 24 laps, accident
312 B2 006	4	Ickx	1:24.4 (2)	3rd, 80 laps
Hockenheim (D), 13 June 1971 (non-championship)				
312 B 003	4	Ickx	1:56.8 (1)	1st, 35 laps; fastest lap, 1:58.8
312 B 004	5	Regazzoni	1:57.7 (2)	14th, 25 laps
Zandvoort (NL), 20 June 1971				
312 B 003	4T; 4	Andretti	1:20.32 (18)	R, 3 laps, fuel pump
312 B 004	3T	Regazzoni	1:18.38	—
312 B2 005	3	Regazzoni	1:17.98 (4)	3rd, 69 laps
312 B2 006	2	Ickx	1:17.42 (1)	1st, 70 laps; fastest lap, 1:34.95
312 B2 007	4	Andretti	1:18.85	—

CHASSIS	NO.	DRIVER(S)	PRACTICE TIME (QUAL. POS.)	RESULT
Paul Ricard (F), 4 July 1971				
312 B2 005	4T	Ickx	—	—
312 B2 005	5T	Regazzoni	1:52.49	—
312 B2 006	4	Ickx	1:51.88 (3)	R, 4 laps, engine
312 B2 007	5	Regazzoni	1:51.53 (2)	R, 20 laps, spin
Silverstone (GB), 17 July 1971				
312 B2 005	5	Regazzoni	1:18.1 (1)	R, 48 laps, engine
312 B2 006	4	Ickx	1:19.5 (6)	R, 51 laps, engine
312 B2 007	34	Ickx	—	—
Nürburgring (D), 1 August 1971				
312 B 004	31	Regazzoni	7:27.6	—
312 B2 005	6	Regazzoni	7:22.7 (4)	3rd, 12 laps
312 B2 006	4	Ickx	7:19.2 (2)	R, 1 lap, accident
312 B2 007	5	Andretti	7:31.7 (11)	4th, 12 laps
Österreichring (A), 15 August 1971				
312 B2 005	5	Regazzoni	1:38.27	—
312 B2 006	4	Ickx	1:38.27 (6)	R, 31 laps, plug leads
312 B2 007	5	Regazzoni	1:37.90 (4)	R, 8 laps, engine
"	6T	Ickx	1:38.87	—
Monza (I), 5 September 1971				
312 B 004	3	Ickx	1:22.82 (2)	R, 15 laps, engine damper
"	4T	Regazzoni	—	—
312 B2 005	4	Regazzoni	1:23.76	—
312 B2 006	3	Ickx	1:24.39	—
312 B2 007	3T	Ickx	—	—
"	4	Regazzoni	1:23.69 (8)	R, 17 laps, engine damper
Mosport (CDN), 19 September 1971				
312 B 004	25T	Regazzoni	1:16.1	—
312 B2 005	5	Regazzoni	1:17.5 (18)	R, 6 laps, accident
312 B2 006	4	Ickx	1:16.5 (12)	8th, 62 laps
312 B2 007	6	Andretti	1:16.9 (13)	13th, 60 laps
Watkins Glen (USA), 3 October 1971				
312 B 004	32	Ickx	1:43.843 (7)	R, 48 laps, alternator; fastest lap, 1:43.47
312 B2 005	5	Regazzoni	1:43.002 (4)	6th, 59 laps
312 B2 006	4	Ickx	1:45.210	—
312 B2 007	6	Andretti	1:43.195	Non-starter, USAC commitment
Buenos Aires (RA), 23 January 1972				
312 B2 005	9	Regazzoni	1:13.28 (6)	4th, 95 laps
312 B2 006	8	Ickx	1:13.50 (8)	3rd, 95 laps
312 B2 007	10	Andretti	1:13.61 (9)	R, 20 laps, misfire
Kyalami (ZA), 4 March 1972				
312 B2 005	6	Regazzoni	1:17.3 (2)	12th, 77 laps
312 B2 006	5	Ickx	1:17.7 (7)	8th, 78 laps
312 B2 007	7	Andretti	1:17.5 (6)	4th, 79 laps
Jarama (E), 1 May 1972				
312 B2 005	7	Andretti	1:19.39 (5)	R, 23 laps, engine
312 B2 006	4	Ickx	1:18.43 (1)	2nd, 90 laps; fastest lap, 1:21.01
312 B2 008	6	Regazzoni	1:19.71 (8)	3rd, 89 laps
Monte Carlo (MC), 14 May 1972				
312 B2 005	7	Regazzoni	1:21.9 (3)	R, 51 laps, accident
312 B2 006	6	Ickx	1:21.6 (2)	2nd, 80 laps
312 B2 008	6T	Ickx	1:31.3	—

CHASSIS	NO.	DRIVER(S)	PRACTICE TIME (QUAL. POS.)	RESULT
Nivelles (B), 4 June 1972				
312 B2 005	30	Regazzoni	1:11.58 (2)	R, 57 laps, accident
312 B2 006	29	Ickx	1:11.84 (4)	R, 47 laps, throttle linkage
312 B2 008	29T	Ickx	—	—
Clermont-Ferrand (F), 2 July 1972				
312 B2 005	3T; 3	Ickx	2:55.1 (4)	11th, 37 laps
312 B2 006	3	Ickx	2:56.8	—
312 B2 007	30	Galli	3:00.7 (19)	13th, 37 laps
Brands Hatch (GB), 15 July 1972				
312 B2 005	5	Ickx	1:22.2 (1)	R, 48 laps, oil radiator leak
312 B2 006	42	Ickx	1:23.6	—
312 B2 007	6	Merzario	1:23.7 (9)	6th, 75 laps
Nürburgring (D), 30 July 1972				
312 B2 005	4	Ickx	7:07.0 (1)	1st, 14 laps; fastest lap, 7:13.6
312 B2 007	9	Regazzoni	7:13.4 (7)	2nd, 14 laps
312 B2 008	19	Merzario	7:25.9 (22)	12th, 13 laps
Österreichring (A), 13 August 1972				
312 B2 005	18	Ickx	1:37.33 (9)	R, 20 laps, fuel pressure
312 B2 006	18T	Ickx	—	—
312 B2 007	19	Regazzoni	1:36.04 (2)	R, 13 laps, fuel pressure
Monza (I), 10 September 1972				
312 B2 005	4	Ickx	1:35.65 (1)	R, 45 laps, electrical failure; fastest lap, 1:36.3
312 B2 007	5	Regazzoni	1:35.83 (4)	R, 16 laps, accident
312 B2 008	3	Andretti	1:36.32 (7)	7th, 54 laps
Mosport (CDN), 24 September 1972				
312 B2 005	10	Ickx	1:14.7 (8)	12th, 76 laps
312 B2 006	10T	Ickx	1:15.4	—
312 B2 007	11	Regazzoni	1:14.5 (7)	5th, 80 laps
Watkins Glen (USA), 8 October 1972				
312 B2 005	7	Ickx	1:42.597 (12)	5th, 59 laps
312 B2 006	9	Andretti	1:42.482 (10)	6th, 58 laps
312 B2 007	8	Regazzoni	1:41.951 (6)	8th, 58 laps
Buenos Aires (RA), 28 January 1973				
312 B2 005	18	Ickx	1:11.01 (3)	4th, 96 laps
312 B2 008	20	Merzario	1:12.54 (14)	9th, 92 laps
Interlagos (BR), 11 February 1973				
312 B2 005	9	Ickx	2:32.0 (3)	5th, 39 laps
312 B2 008	10	Merzario	2:37.7 (17)	4th, 39 laps
Kyalami (ZA), 3 March 1973				
312 B2 005	9	Merzario	1:17.64 (15)	4th, 78 laps
312 B2 006	8	Ickx	1:17.16 (11)	R, 1 lap, accident
Barcelona (E), 29 April 1973				
312 B3 010	7	Ickx	1:23.5 (6)	12th, 69 laps
312 B3 011	8	Ickx	1:46.9	—
Zolder (B), 20 May 1973				
312 B3 010	3T	Ickx	—	—
312 B3 011	3	Ickx	1:23.10 (3)	R, 5 laps, oil pump
Monte Carlo (MC), 3 June 1973				
312 B3 010	3	Ickx	1:28.7 (7)	R, 44 laps, driveshaft
312 B3 011	4	Merzario	1:29.5 (16)	R, 58 laps, oil pressure

CHASSIS	NO.	DRIVER(S)	PRACTICE TIME (QUAL. POS.)	RESULT
Anderstorp (S), 17 June 1973				
312 B3 010	3	Ickx	1:25.604 (12)	6th 79 laps
312 B3 011	3T	Ickx	—	—
Paul Ricard (F), 1 July 1973				
312 B3 010	3	Ickx	1:51.44 (12)	5th, 54 laps
312 B3 011	3T	Ickx	1:51.92	—
312 B3 012	4	Merzario	1:51.17 (10)	7th, 54 laps
Silverstone (GB), 14 July 1973				
312 B3 010	3	Ickx	1:18.9 (19)	8th, 67 laps
312 B3 012	3T	Ickx	—	—
Österreichring (A), 19 August 1973				
312 B3 S 011	4	Merzario	1:36.42 (6)	7th, 53 laps
Monza (I), 9 September 1973				
312 B3 S 010	3	Ickx	1:36.99 (14)	R, 1 lap, accident
312 B3 S 011	4	Merzario	1:36.37 (7)	8th, 54 laps
Mosport (CDN), 23 September 1973				
312 B3 S 011	4	Merzario	1:17.350 (20)	15th, 75 laps
Watkins Glen (USA), 7 October 1973				
312 B3 S 011	4	Merzario	1:41.455 (11)	16th, 55 laps
Buenos Aires (RA), 13 January 1974				
312 B3 011	11	Regazzoni	1:50.96 (2)	3rd, 53 laps; fastest lap, 1:52.10
312 B3 012	12	Lauda	1:51.81 (8)	2nd, 53 laps
Interlagos (BR), 27 January 1974				
312 B3 011	11	Regazzoni	2:35.05 (8)	2nd, 32 laps; fastest lap, 2:36.05
312 B3 012	12	Lauda	2:33.77 (3)	R, 2 laps, broken wing
Brands Hatch (GB), 17 March 1974 (non-championship)				
312 B3 010	12	Lauda	1:22.1 (3)	2nd, 40 laps
312 B3 011	11	Regazzoni	1:21.6 (2)	5th, 40 laps
Kyalami (ZA), 30 March 1974				
312 B3 011	11	Regazzoni	1:16.85 (6)	R, 64 laps, oil pressure
312 B3 012	12	Lauda	1:16.58 (1)	16th, 74 laps, not running at finish
Jarama (E), 28 April 1974				
312 B3 014	11	Regazzoni	1:18.78 (3)	2nd, 84 laps
312 B3 015	12	Lauda	1:18.44 (1)	1st, 84 laps; fastest lap, 1:20.33
Nivelles (B), 12 May 1974				
312 B3 010	11T	Regazzoni	1:09.82 (1)	—
312 B3 011	11	Regazzoni	1:11.68	4th, 85 laps
312 B3 012	12	Lauda	1:11.04 (3)	2nd, 85 laps
Monte Carlo (MC), 26 May 1974				
312 B3 010	11T	Regazzoni	—	—
"	12	Lauda	1:26.3 (1)	R, 31 laps, ignition
312 B3 012	11T	Regazzoni	1:31.6	—
"	12T	Lauda	—	—
312 B3 014	11	Regazzoni	1:26.6 (2)	4th, 78 laps
312 B3 015	12T	Lauda	—	—
Anderstorp (S), 9 June 1974				
312 B3 011	11	Regazzoni	1:25.276 (4)	R, 22 laps, transmission
312 B3 012	11T	Regazzoni	1:45.504	—
312 B3 015	12	Lauda	1:25.161 (3)	R, 68 laps, transmission

CHASSIS	NO.	DRIVER(S)	PRACTICE TIME (QUAL. POS.)	RESULT
Zandvoort (NL), 23 June 1974				
312 B3 014	11	Regazzoni	1:18.91 (2)	2nd, 75 laps
312 B3 015	12	Lauda	1:18.31 (1)	1st, 75 laps
Dijon (F), 7 July 1974				
312 B3 011	11T	Regazzoni	1:00.14	—
312 B3 012	12	Lauda	0:58.79 (1)	2nd, 80 laps
312 B3 014	11	Regazzoni	0:59.13 (4)	3rd, 80 laps
Brands Hatch (GB), 20 July 1974				
312 B3 014	11	Regazzoni	1:20.3 (7)	4th, 75 laps
312 B3 015	12	Lauda	1:19.7 (1)	5th, 74 laps (initially classified 9th); fastest lap, 1:21.1
Nürburgring (D), 4 August 1974				
312 B3 012	12	Lauda	7:00.8 (1)	R, 0 laps, accident
312 B3 014	—	—	—	—
312 B3 016	11	Regazzoni	7:01.1 (2)	1st, 14 laps
Österreichring (A), 18 August 1974				
312 B3 011	11T	Regazzoni	1:36.43	—
"	12T	Lauda	1:36.22	—
312 B3 014	11	Regazzoni	1:36.31 (8)	5th, 54 laps; fastest lap, 1:37.22
312 B3 015	12	Lauda	1:35.40 (1)	R, 16 laps, engine
Monza (I), 8 September 1974				
312 B3 014	11	Regazzoni	1:33.73 (5)	R, 38 laps, engine
312 B3 015	12	Lauda	1:33.16 (1)	R, 30 laps, engine
Mosport (CDN), 22 September 1974				
312 B3 014	11T	Regazzoni	1:13.582	—
"	12T	Lauda	1:14.575	—
312 B3 015	12	Lauda	1:13.230 (2)	R, 66 laps, accident; fastest lap, 1:13.659
312 B3 016	11	Regazzoni	1:13.553 (6)	2nd, 80 laps
Watkins Glen (USA), 6 October 1974				
312 B3 010	12T	Lauda	1:39.989	—
312 B3 011	11	Regazzoni	1:39.600 (9)	11th, 55 laps
312 B3 014	12	Lauda	1:39.327 (5)	R, 37 laps, suspension
Buenos Aires (RA), 12 January 1975				
312 B3 012	11T	Regazzoni	—	—
312 B3 014	11	Regazzoni	1:50.71 (7)	4th, 53 laps
312 B3 020	12	Lauda	1:49.96 (4)	6th, 53 laps
Interlagos (BR), 26 January 1975				
312 B3 012	12T	Lauda	2:32.97	—
312 B3 014	11	Regazzoni	2:31.22 (5)	4th, 40 laps
312 B3 020	12	Lauda	2:31.12 (4)	5th, 40 laps
Kyalami (ZA), 1 March 1975				
312 B3 014	12T	Lauda	1:16.96	—
312 T 018	12	Lauda	1:16.83 (4)	5th, 78 laps
312 T 021	11	Regazzoni	1:17.16 (9)	R, 71 laps, throttle linkage
Silverstone (GB), 13 April 1975 (non-championship)				
312 T 022	12	Lauda	1:17.4 (2)	1st, 40 laps
Barcelona (E), 27 April 1975				
312 T 021	11	Regazzoni	1:23.5 (2)	11th, 25 laps
312 T 022	12	Lauda	1:23.4 (1)	R, 0 laps, accident

CHASSIS	NO.	DRIVER(S)	PRACTICE TIME (QUAL. POS.)	RESULT
Monte Carlo (MC), 11 May 1975				
312 T 018	11T	Regazzoni	1:28.22	—
"	12T	Lauda	1:28.57	—
312 T 021	11	Regazzoni	1:27.55 (6)	R, 36 laps, accident
"	12T	Lauda	1:27.62	—
312 T 023	12	Lauda	1:26.40 (1)	1st, 75 laps
Zolder (B), 25 May 1975				
312 T 018	—	—	—	—
312 T 022	11	Regazzoni	1:25.85 (4)	5th, 70 laps; fastest lap, 1:26.76
312 T 023	12	Lauda	1:25.43 (1)	1st, 70 laps
Anderstorp (S), 8 June 1975				
312 T 018	12T	Lauda	—	—
312 T 021	11	Regazzoni	1:26.283 (12)	3rd, 80 laps
312 T 023	12	Lauda	1:25.457 (5)	1st, 80 laps; fastest lap, 1:28.267
Zandvoort (NL), 22 June 1975				
312 T 018	—	—	—	—
312 T 021	11	Regazzoni	1:20.57 (2)	3rd, 75 laps
312 T 022	12	Lauda	1:20.29 (1)	2nd, 75 laps; fastest lap, 1:21.54
Paul Ricard (F), 6 July 1975				
312 T 018	12T	Lauda	—	—
312 T 022	12	Lauda	1:47.82 (1)	1st, 54 laps
312 T 024	11	Regazzoni	1:48.68 (9)	R, 6 laps, engine
Silverstone (GB), 19 July 1975				
312 T 021	—	—	—	—
312 T 023	12	Lauda	1:19.54 (3)	8th, 54 laps
312 T 024	11	Regazzoni	1:19.55 (4)	13th, 54 laps; fastest lap, 1:20.9
Nürburgring (D), 3 August 1975				
312 T 018	—	—	—	—
312 T 021	11	Regazzoni	7:01.6 (5)	R, 9 laps, engine; fastest lap, 7:06.4
312 T 022	12	Lauda	6:58.6 (1)	3rd, 14 laps
Österreichring (A), 17 August 1975				
312 T 022	12	Lauda	1:34.85 (1)	6th, 29 laps
312 T 023	11T	Regazzoni	1:36.71	—
312 T 024	11	Regazzoni	1:35.41 (5)	7th, 29 laps
Dijon (F), 24 August 1975 (non-championship)				
312 T 021	11	Regazzoni	0:59.76 (3)	1st, 60 laps
Monza (I), 7 September 1975				
312 T 021	11T	Regazzoni	1:32.75 (2)	—
312 T 023	12	Lauda	1:32.24 (1)	3rd, 52 laps
312 T 024	11	Regazzoni	1:32.79	1st, 52 laps; fastest lap, 1:33.1
Watkins Glen (USA), 5 October 1975				
312 T 022	12T	Lauda	1:42.173	—
"	11T	Regazzoni	1:43.857	—
312 T 023	12	Lauda	1:42.003 (1)	1st, 59 laps
312 T 024	11	Regazzoni	1:43.246 (11)	R, 28 laps, withdrawn
Interlagos (BR), 25 January 1976				
312 T 023	1	Lauda	2:32.52 (2)	1st, 40 laps
312 T 024	2	Regazzoni	2:33.17 (4)	7th, 40 laps

CHASSIS	NO.	DRIVER(S)	PRACTICE TIME (QUAL. POS.)	RESULT
Kyalami (ZA), 6 March 1976				
312 T 022	2T; 2	Regazzoni	1:16.94 (10)	R, 52 laps, engine
312 T 023	1	Lauda	1:16.20 (2)	1st, 78 laps; fastest lap, 1:17.94
312 T 024	2	Regazzoni	—	—
Brands Hatch (GB), 14 March 1976 (non-championship)				
312 T2 025	1	Lauda	1:22.77 (2)	R, 16 laps, brake pipe
Long Beach (USA), 28 March 1976				
312 T 022	1T	Lauda	—	—
312 T 023	1	Lauda	1:23.647 (4)	2nd, 80 laps
312 T 024	2	Regazzoni	1:23.099 (1)	1st, 80 laps; fastest lap, 1:23.076
Jarama (E), 2 May 1976				
312 T2 025	2	Regazzoni	1:19.15 (5)	10th, 72 laps
312 T2 026	1	Lauda	1:18.84 (2)	2nd, 75 laps
Zolder (B), 16 May 1976				
312 T2 023*	1T	Lauda	—	—
312 T2 025	2	Regazzoni	1:26.60 (2)	2nd, 70 laps
312 T2 026	1	Lauda	1:26.55 (1)	1st, 70 laps; fastest lap, 1:25.98

*Converted 312 T

CHASSIS	NO.	DRIVER(S)	PRACTICE TIME (QUAL. POS.)	RESULT
Monte Carlo (MC), 30 May 1976				
312 T2 025	1T	Lauda	1:31.13	—
"	2T	Regazzoni	—	—
312 T2 026	1	Lauda	1:29.65 (1)	1st, 78 laps; fastest lap, 1:30.36
312 T2 027	2	Regazzoni	1:29.91 (2)	R, 73 laps, accident
Anderstorp (S), 13 June 1976				
312 T2 025	2T	Regazzoni	—	—
312 T2 026	1	Lauda	1:26.441 (5)	3rd, 72 laps
312 T2 027	2	Regazzoni	1:27.157 (11)	6th, 72 laps
Paul Ricard (F), 4 July 1976				
312 T2 025*	1T	Lauda	—	—
312 T2 026	1	Lauda	1:48.17 (2)	R, 8 laps, engine; fastest lap, 1:51.0
312 T2 027	2	Regazzoni	1:48.69 (4)	R, 17 laps, engine

*De Dion rear suspension

CHASSIS	NO.	DRIVER(S)	PRACTICE TIME (QUAL. POS.)	RESULT
Brands Hatch (GB), 18 July 1976				
312 T2 026	2T; 2	Regazzoni	—	R, 36 laps, engine (second start)
312 T2 027	2	Regazzoni	1:20.05 (4)	Accident in first start
312 T2 028	1	Lauda	1:19.35 (1)	1st, 76 laps (initially classified 2nd)
Nürburgring (D), 1 August 1976				
312 T2 025	2	Regazzoni	7:09.3 (5)	9th, 14 laps
312 T2 028	1	Lauda	7:07.4 (2)	R, 2 laps, accident
Zandvoort (NL), 29 August 1976				
312 T2 026	2T	Regazzoni	—	—
312 T2 027	2	Regazzoni	1:21.85 (5)	2nd, 75 laps
Monza (I), 12 September 1976				
312 T2 025	35	Reutemann	1:42.38 (7)	9th, 52 laps
312 T2 026	1	Lauda	1:42.09 (5)	4th, 52 laps
312 T2 027	2	Regazzoni	1:42.96 (9)	2nd, 52 laps
Mosport (CDN), 3 October 1976				
312 T2 026	1	Lauda	1:13.060 (6)	8th, 80 laps
312 T2 027	2	Regazzoni	1:13.500 (12)	6th, 80 laps
312 T2 028	—	—	—	—

156

CHASSIS	NO.	DRIVER(S)	PRACTICE TIME (QUAL. POS.)	RESULT
Watkins Glen (USA), 10 October 1976				
312 T2 026	1	Lauda	1:44.257 (5)	3rd, 59 laps
312 T2 027	2	Regazzoni	1:45.534 (14)	7th, 58 laps
Fuji (J), 24 October 1976				
312 T2 026	1	Lauda	1:13.08 (3)	R, 2 laps, driver decision
312 T2 027	2	Regazzoni	1:13.64 (7)	5th, 72 laps
Buenos Aires (RA), 9 January 1977				
312 T2 026	11	Lauda	1:49.73 (4)	R, 20 laps, engine
312 T2 027	11T	Lauda	1:51.03	—
312 T2 029	12	Reutemann	1:50.02 (7)	3rd, 53 laps
Interlagos (BR), 23 January 1977				
312 T2 026	11	Lauda	2:32.37 (13)	3rd, 40 laps
312 T2 027	11T	Lauda	2:33.48	—
312 T2 029	12	Reutemann	2:30.18 (2)	1st, 40 laps
Kyalami (ZA), 5 March 1977				
312 T2 027	12T	Reutemann	—	—
312 T2 029	12	Reutemann	1:16.54 (8)	8th, 78 laps
312 T2 030	11	Lauda	1:16.29 (3)	1st, 78 laps
Long Beach (USA), 3 April 1977				
312 T2 027	11T	Lauda	—	—
312 T2 029	12	Reutemann	1:22.260 (4)	R, 5 laps, accident
312 T2 030	11	Lauda	1:21.630 (1)	2nd, 80 laps; fastest lap, 1:21.650
Jarama (E), 8 May 1977				
312 T2 029	12	Reutemann	1:19.52 (4)	2nd, 75 laps
312 T2 030	11	Lauda	1:19.48 (3)	Non-starter, injury
Monte Carlo (MC), 22 May 1977				
312 T2 029	12	Reutemann	1:30.44 (3)	3rd, 76 laps
312 T2 030	11	Lauda	1:30.76 (6)	2nd, 76 laps
Zolder (B), 5 June 1977				
312 T2 029	12	Reutemann	1:26.85 (7)	R, 14 laps, accident
312 T2 030	11	Lauda	1:27.11 (11)	2nd, 70 laps
Anderstorp (S), 19 June 1977				
312 T2 027	11T	Lauda	1:26.873	—
"	12T; 12	Reutemann	1:26.542 (12)	3rd, 72 laps
312 T2 029	12	Reutemann	1:27.002	—
312 T2 030	11	Lauda	1:26.826 (15)	R, 47 laps, handling
Dijon (F), 3 July 1977				
312 T2 029	12	Reutemann	1:13.36 (6)	6th, 79 laps
312 T2 031	11	Lauda	1:13.52 (9)	5th, 80 laps
Silverstone (GB), 16 July 1977				
312 T2 029	12	Reutemann	1:19.64 (14)	14th, 62 laps
312 T2 031	11	Lauda	1:18.84 (3)	2nd, 68 laps
Hockenheim (D), 31 July 1977				
312 T2 029	12	Reutemann	1:54.27 (6)	4th, 47 laps
312 T2 031	11	Lauda	1:53.53 (3)	1st, 47 laps; fastest lap, 1:55.99
Österreichring (A), 14 August 1977				
312 T2 029	12	Reutemann	1:40.12 (5)	4th, 54 laps
312 T2 030	12T	Reutemann	—	—
312 T2 031	11	Lauda	1:39.32 (1)	2nd, 54 laps

CHASSIS	NO.	DRIVER(S)	PRACTICE TIME (QUAL. POS.)	RESULT
Zandvoort (NL), 28 August 1977				
312 T2 029	12	Reutemann	1:19.66 (6)	6th, 73 laps
312 T2 030	11	Lauda	1:19.54 (4)	1st, 75 laps; Fastest lap, 1:19.99
312 T2 031	11T	Lauda	—	—
Monza (I), 11 September 1977				
312 T2 029	12	Reutemann	1:38.15 (2)	R, 39 laps, spin
312 T2 030	12T	Reutemann	—	—
312 T2 031	11	Lauda	1:38.54 (5)	2nd, 52 laps
Watkins Glen (USA), 2 October 1977				
312 T2 029	12T	Reutemann	—	—
312 T2 030	12	Reutemann	1:41.952 (6)	6th, 58 laps
312 T2 031	11	Lauda	1:42.089 (7)	4th, 59 laps
Mosport (CDN), 9 October 1977				
312 T2 029	12	Reutemann	1:13.890 (12)	R, 20 laps, fuel pressure
312 T2 030	21	Villeneuve	1:14.465 (17)	12th, 76 laps, not running at finish
312 T2 031	11	Lauda	Did not practice	—
Fuji (J), 23 October 1977				
312 T2 029	12	Reutemann	1:13.32 (7)	2nd, 73 laps
312 T2 030	11	Villeneuve	1:14.51 (20)	R, 5 laps, accident
312 T2 031	12T	Reutemann	—	—
Buenos Aires (RA), 15 January 1978				
312 T2 027	12	Villeneuve	1:48.97 (7)	8th, 52 laps; fastest lap, 1:49.76
312 T2 029	11T	Reutemann	—	—
312 T2 031	11	Reutemann	1:47.84 (2)	7th, 52 laps
Rio (BR), 29 January 1978				
312 T2 027	12	Villeneuve	1:40.97 (6)	R, 35 laps, accident
312 T2 029	11T	Reutemann	—	—
312 T2 031	11	Reutemann	1:40.73 (4)	1st, 63 laps; fastest lap, 1:43.07
Kyalami (ZA), 4 March 1978				
312 T3 032	12	Villeneuve	1:15.50 (8)	R, 55 laps, oil leak
312 T3 033	11	Reutemann	1:15.52 (9)	R, 55 laps, accident
Long Beach (USA), 2 April 1978				
312 T3 032	11	Reutemann	1:20.636 (1)	1st, 80½ laps
312 T3 033	11T	Reutemann	—	—
312 T3 034	12	Villeneuve	1:20.836 (2)	R, 38 laps, accident
Monte Carlo (MC), 7 May 1978				
312 T3 032	12	Villeneuve	1:29.40 (8)	R, 62 laps, accident
312 T3 034	11	Reutemann	1:28.34 (1)	8th, 74 laps
312 T3 035	11T	Reutemann	—	—
Zolder (B), 21 May 1978				
312 T3 033	11T; 11	Reutemann	1:21.69 (2)	3rd, 70 laps
312 T3 034	12	Villeneuve	1:21.77 (4)	4th, 70 laps
312 T3 035	11	Reutemann	1:22.60	—
Jarama (E), 4 June 1978				
312 T3 033	11T	Reutemann	—	—
312 T3 034	12	Villeneuve	1:17.76 (5)	10th, 74 laps
312 T3 035	11	Reutemann	1:17.40 (3)	R, 57 laps, accident
Anderstorp (S), 17 June 1978				
312 T3 034	12	Villeneuve	1:23.730 (7)	9th, 69 laps
312 T3 035	11T	Reutemann	—	—
312 T3 036	11	Reutemann	1:23.737 (8)	10th, 69 laps

CHASSIS	NO.	DRIVER(S)	PRACTICE TIME (QUAL. POS.)	RESULT
Paul Ricard (F), 2 July 1978				
312 T3 034	12	Villeneuve	1:45.55 (9)	12th, 53 laps
312 T3 035	11T	Reutemann	—	—
312 T3 036	11	Reutemann	1:45.35 (8)	18th, 49 laps; fastest lap, 1:48.56
Brands Hatch (GB), 16 July 1978				
312 T3 033	11	Reutemann	1:18.45 (8)	1st, 76 laps
312 T3 034	12	Villeneuve	1:18.99 (13)	R, 19 laps, driveshaft
312 T3 035	11T	Reutemann	—	—
Hockenheim (D), 30 July 1978				
312 T3 033	11T	Reutemann	1:54.17 (12)	—
312 T3 034	12	Villeneuve	1:54.40 (15)	8th, 45 laps
312 T3 035	11	Reutemann	—	R, 14 laps, fuel pressure
Österreichring (A), 13 August 1978				
312 T3 034	12	Villeneuve	1:39.40 (11)	3rd, 54 laps
312 T3 035	11T	Reutemann	1:38.61	—
312 T3 036	11	Reutemann	1:38.50 (4)	R, 27 laps, disqualified for push start
Zandvoort (NL), 27 August 1978				
312 T3 034	12	Villeneuve	1:17.54 (5)	6th, 75 laps
312 T3 035	11T	Reutemann	—	—
"	12T	Villeneuve	—	—
312 T3 036	11	Reutemann	1:17.34 (4)	7th, 75 laps
Monza (I), 10 September 1978				
312 T3 034	12	Villeneuve	1:37.866 (2)	7th, 40 laps (finished 2nd, penalized 1 min.)
312 T3 035	11T	Reutemann	1:38.969	3rd, 40 laps (second start)
"	12T	Villeneuve	1:39.046	—
312 T3 036	11	Reutemann	1:38.959 (11)	Accident in first start
Watkins Glen (USA), 1 October 1978				
312 T3 034	12	Villeneuve	1:39.820 (4)	R, 22 laps, engine
312 T3 035	11	Reutemann	1:39.179 (2)	1st, 59 laps
312 T3 036	11T	Reutemann	—	—
Montreal (CDN), 8 October 1978				
312 T3 034	12	Villeneuve	1:38.230 (3)	1st, 70 laps
312 T3 035	11	Reutemann	1:39.455 (11)	3rd, 70 laps
312 T3 036	11T	Reutemann	—	—
Buenos Aires (RA), 21 January 1979				
312 T3 033	11T	Scheckter	—	—
312 T3 033	12T	Villeneuve	—	—
312 T3 035	11	Scheckter	1:45.58 (5)	R, 0 laps, accident
312 T3 036	12	Villeneuve	1:46.88 (10)	12th, 48 laps, not running at finish
Interlagos (BR), 4 February 1979				
312 T3 034	12	Villeneuve	2:24.34 (5)	5th, 39 laps
312 T3 035	11	Scheckter	2:24.48 (6)	6th, 39 laps
312 T3 036	12T	Villeneuve	—	—
Kyalami (ZA), 3 March 1979				
312 T3 033	—	—	—	—
312 T4 037	12	Villeneuve	1:12.07 (3)	1st, 78 laps; fastest lap, 1:14.41
312 T4 038	11	Scheckter	1:12.04 (2)	2nd, 78 laps
Long Beach (USA), 8 April 1979				
312 T4 037	12	Villeneuve	1:18.825 (1)	1st, 80½ laps; fastest lap, 1:21.20
312 T4 038	11	Scheckter	1:18.911 (3)	2nd, 80½ laps
312 T4 039	11T	Scheckter	—	—

CHASSIS	NO.	DRIVER(S)	PRACTICE TIME (QUAL. POS.)	RESULT
Brands Hatch (GB), 15 April 1979 (non-championship)				
312 T3 033	12	Villeneuve	1:17.85 (3)	1st, 40 laps
Jarama (E), 29 April 1979				
312 T4 037	12	Villeneuve	1:14.83 (3)	7th, 75 laps; fastest lap, 1:16.44
312 T4 038	11T	Scheckter	1:15.10 (5)	—
312 T3 039	11	Scheckter	1:15.60	4th, 75 laps
Zolder (B), 13 May 1979				
312 T4 038	12T	Villeneuve	—	—
312 T4 039	12	Villeneuve	1:22.08 (6)	7th, 69 laps
312 T4 040	11	Scheckter	1:22.08 (7)	1st, 70 laps; fastest lap, 1:22.39
Monte Carlo (MC), 27 May 1979				
312 T4 038	12T	Villeneuve	—	—
312 T4 039	12	Villeneuve	1:26.52 (2)	R, 53 laps, transmission
312 T4 040	11	Scheckter	1:26.43 (1)	1st, 76 laps
Dijon (F), 1 July 1979				
312 T4 037	11T	Scheckter	—	—
312 T4 040	11	Scheckter	1:08.15 (5)	7th, 79 laps
312 T4 041	12	Villeneuve	1:07.65 (3)	2nd, 80 laps
Silverstone (GB), 14 July 1979				
312 T4 037	11T	Scheckter	1:15.30	—
"	12T	Villeneuve	1:14.92	—
312 T4 038	12	Villeneuve	1:14.90 (13)	14th, 63 laps, not running at finish
312 T4 039	11	Scheckter	1:14.60 (11)	5th, 67 laps
Hockenheim (D), 29 July 1979				
312 T4 039	12T	Villeneuve	—	—
312 T4 040	11	Scheckter	1:50.00 (5)	4th, 45 laps
312 T4 041	12	Villeneuve	1:50.41 (9)	8th, 44 laps; fastest lap, 1:51.89
Österreichring (A), 12 August 1979				
312 T4 038	11T	Scheckter	—	—
"	12T	Villeneuve	—	—
312 T4 040	11	Scheckter	1:36.10 (9)	4th, 54 laps
312 T4 041	12	Villeneuve	1:35.70 (5)	2nd, 54 laps
Zandvoort (NL), 26 August 1979				
312 T4 039	12T	Villeneuve	—	—
312 T4 040	11	Scheckter	1:16.392 (5)	2nd, 75 laps
312 T4 041	12	Villeneuve	1:16.939 (6)	R, 49 laps, tire
Monza (I), 9 September 1979				
312 T4B 037	11T	Scheckter	—	—
312 T4 038	12	Villeneuve	1:34.989 (5)	2nd, 50 laps
312 T4 040	11	Scheckter	1:34.830 (3)	1st, 50 laps
312 T4B 041	12T	Villeneuve	1:35.365	—
Imola (I), 16 September 1979 (non-championship)				
312 T4B 038	12	Villeneuve	1:32.910 (1)	7th, 40 laps; fastest lap, 1:33.61
312 T4B 040	11	Scheckter	1:33.240 (2)	3rd, 40 laps
Montreal (CDN), 30 September 1979				
312 T4B 038	12T	Villeneuve	—	—
312 T4 040	11	Scheckter	1:32.280 (9)	4th, 71 laps
312 T4 041	12	Villeneuve	1:30.554 (2)	2nd, 72 laps

CHASSIS	NO.	DRIVER(S)	PRACTICE TIME (QUAL. POS.)	RESULT
Watkins Glen (USA), 7 October 1979				
312 T4 038	11T	Scheckter	—	—
312 T4 040	11	Scheckter	1:39.576 (16)	R, 48 laps, puncture
312 T4 041	12	Villeneuve	1:36.948 (3)	1st, 59 laps
Buenos Aires (RA), 13 January 1980				
312 T5 042	1	Scheckter	1:46.28 (11)	R, 45 laps, engine
312 T5 043	2	Villeneuve	1:46.07 (8)	R, 36 laps, suspension
312 T5 044	1T	Scheckter	—	—
Interlagos (BR), 27 January 1980				
312 T5 042	1	Scheckter	2:23.02 (8)	R, 10 laps, oil pressure
312 T5 044	2T	Villeneuve	—	—
312 T5 045	2	Villeneuve	2:22.17 (3)	16th, 36 laps, not running at finish
Kyalami (ZA), 1 March 1980				
312 T5 042	2	Villeneuve	1:12.38 (10)	R, 31 laps, transmission
312 T5 045	2T	Villeneuve	—	—
312 T5 046	1	Scheckter	1:12.32 (9)	R, 13 laps, engine
Long Beach (USA), 30 March 1980				
312 T5 042	1T	Scheckter	—	—
312 T5 045	2	Villeneuve	1:19.285 (10)	R, 45 laps, driveshaft
312 T5 046	1	Scheckter	1:20.151 (16)	5th, 79 laps
Zolder (B), 4 May 1980				
312 T5 045	2	Villeneuve	1:21.54 (12)	6th, 71 laps
312 T5 046	1	Scheckter	1:21.58 (14)	8th, 71 laps
Monte Carlo (MC), 18 May 1980				
312 T5 044	2T	Villeneuve	—	—
312 T5 045*	2	Villeneuve	1:26.104 (6)	5th, 75 laps
312 T5 046*	1	Scheckter	1:27.182 (17)	R, 27 laps, handling

*Short wheelbase

CHASSIS	NO.	DRIVER(S)	PRACTICE TIME (QUAL. POS.)	RESULT
Jarama (E), 1 June 1980*				
312 T5 044	2	Villeneuve	Withdrawn; did not practice or race	
312 T5 046	1	Scheckter	Withdrawn; did not practice or race	

*Event subsequently nullified

CHASSIS	NO.	DRIVER(S)	PRACTICE TIME (QUAL. POS.)	RESULT
Paul Ricard (F), 29 June 1980				
312 T5 044	1T	Scheckter	—	—
312 T5 045	2	Villeneuve	1:41.99 (17)	8th, 53 laps
312 T5 046	1	Scheckter	1:42.38 (19)	12th, 52 laps
Brands Hatch (GB), 13 July 1980				
312 T5 044	1T	Scheckter	—	—
312 T5 046	1	Scheckter	1:15.370 (23)	10th, 73 laps
312 T5 048	2	Villeneuve	1:14.296 (19)	R, 35 laps, engine
Hockenheim (D), 10 August 1980				
312 T5 046	1	Scheckter	1:49.35 (21)	13th, 44 laps
312 T5 048	2	Villeneuve	1:48.86 (16)	6th, 45 laps
Österreichring (A), 17 August 1980				
312 T5 043	2	Villeneuve	1:34.87 (15)	8th, 53 laps
312 T5 044	1	Scheckter	1:35.61 (22)	13th, 53 laps
312 T5 045	2T	Villeneuve	—	—
Zandvoort (NL), 31 August 1980				
312 T5 046	1	Scheckter	1:18.87 (12)	10th, 70 laps
312 T5 048	2	Villeneuve	1:18.40 (7)	7th, 71 laps

CHASSIS	NO.	DRIVER(S)	PRACTICE TIME (QUAL. POS.)	RESULT

Imola (I), 14 September 1980

CHASSIS	NO.	DRIVER(S)	PRACTICE TIME (QUAL. POS.)	RESULT
312 T5 043	1T; 1	Scheckter	—	8th, 59 laps
312 T5 046	1	Scheckter	1:36.827 (16)	—
312 T5 048	2	Villeneuve	1:36.350 (8)*	R, 5 laps, accident

*Starting position earned with 2T, 126C turbo chassis 049, 1:35.751

Montreal (CDN), 28 September 1980

312 T5 043	1	Scheckter	1:31.688	Non-starter, did not qualify
312 T5 044	2T	Villeneuve	—	—
312 T5 045	2	Villeneuve	1:30.855 (22)	5th, 70 laps

Watkins Glen (USA), 5 October 1980

312 T5 043	2	Villeneuve	1:37.040 (18)	R, 49 laps, accident
312 T5 044	1	Scheckter	1:38.149 (22)	10th, 56 laps
312 T5 045	2T	Villeneuve	—	—

312 PB

Buenos Aires 1000-Km (RA), 10 January 1971

| 312 PB 0880 | 24 | Giunti/Merzario | 1:52.74 (2) | R, 38 laps, accident |

Sebring 12-Hours (USA), 21 March 1971

| 312 PB 0878 | 25 | Ickx/Andretti | 2:32.47 (2) | R, 117 laps, transmission |

Brands Hatch 1000-Km (GB), 4 April 1971

| 312 PB 0878 | 51 | Ickx/Regazzoni | 1:27.4 (1) | 2nd, 232 laps |

Monza 1000-Km (I), 25 April 1971

| 312 PB 0876 | 15 | Ickx/Regazzoni | 1:33.93 (2) | R, 12 laps, accident |

Spa-Francorchamps 1000-Km (B), 9 May 1971

| 312 PB 0876 | 1 | Ickx/Regazzoni | 3:22.2 (5) | 8th, 54 laps, not running at finish |

Nürburgring 1000-Km (D), 30 May 1971

| 312 PB 0876 | 15 | Ickx/Regazzoni | 7:36.1 (1) | R, 21 laps, overheating; fastest lap, 7:40.8 |

Österreichring 1000-Km (A), 27 June 1971

| 312 PB 0876 | 7 | Ickx/Regazzoni | 1:40.10 (2) | R, 148 laps, accident |

Watkins Glen 6-Hours (USA), 24 July 1971

| 312 PB 0878 | 40 | Ickx/Andretti | 1:08.64 (3) | R, 55 laps, starter motor |

Imola (I), 12 September 1971 (non-championship, two heats)

| 312 PB 0878 | — | Regazzoni | 1:29.47 (2) | 1st/11th = 11th, 36 laps; fastest lap, 1:41.6 |

Kyalami 9-Hours (ZA), 6 November 1971 (non-championship)

| 312 PB 0878 | 6 | Regazzoni/Redman | 1:19.7 (1) | 1st, 355 laps |
| 312 PB 0884 | 5 | Ickx/Andretti | 1:20.3 (2) | 2nd, 340 laps; fastest lap, 1:20.1 |

Buenos Aires 1000-Km (RA), 9 January 1972

312 PB 0882	28	Ickx/Andretti	1:58.98 (3)	10th, 152 laps
312 PB 0884	32	Regazzoni/Redman	1:59.15 (4)	2nd, 168 laps
312 PB 0886	30	Peterson/Schenken	1:58.59 (1)	1st, 168 laps

Daytona 6-Hours (USA), 6 February 1972

312 PB 0888	2	Ickx/Andretti	1:44.22 (1)	1st, 194 laps
312 PB 0890	4	Regazzoni/Redman	1:44.96 (2)	4th, 179 laps; fastest lap, 1:45.00
312 PB 0892	6	Peterson/Schenken	1:46.04 (3)	2nd, 192 laps

CHASSIS	NO.	DRIVER(S)	PRACTICE TIME (QUAL. POS.)	RESULT
Sebring 12-Hours (USA), 25 March 1972				
312 PB 0882	2	Ickx/Andretti	2:31.44 (1)	1st, 259 laps
312 PB 0884	4	Regazzoni/Redman	2:33.04 (2)	R, 215 laps, fire
312 PB 0886	3	Peterson/Schenken	2:35.37 (4)	2nd, 257 laps; fastest lap, 2:33.8
Brands Hatch 1000-Km (GB), 16 April 1972				
312 PB 0888	11	Ickx/Andretti	1:26.8 (2)	1st, 235 laps; fastest lap, 1:27.4*
312 PB 0890	9	Regazzoni/Redman	1:26.6 (1)	5th, 220 laps; fastest lap*
312 PB 0894	10	Peterson/Schenken	1:27.4 (3)	2nd, 234 laps; fastest lap*

*Lap time shared by all three cars

CHASSIS	NO.	DRIVER(S)	PRACTICE TIME (QUAL. POS.)	RESULT
Monza 1000-Km (I), 25 April 1972				
312 PB 0882	1	Ickx/Andretti	1:24.98 (2)	1st, 174 laps
312 PB 0884	3	Redman/Merzario	1:25.59 (3)	R, 33 laps, accident
312 PB 0886	2	Peterson/Schenken	1:24.75 (1)	3rd, 165 laps; fastest lap, 1:46.1
Spa-Francorchamps 1000-Km (B), 7 May 1972				
312 PB 0886	2	Peterson/Schenken	3:25.4 (3)	12th, 56 laps, not running at finish
312 PB 0888	1	Ickx/Regazzoni	3:20.4 (1)	2nd, 70 laps; fastest lap, 3:20.7
312 PB 0890	3	Redman/Merzario	3:23.5 (2)	1st, 71 laps
Targa Florio (I), 21 May 1972				
312 PB 0884	3	Merzario/Munari	33:59.7 (1)	1st, 11 laps
Nürburgring 1000-Km (D), 28 May 1972				
312 PB 0882	1	Ickx/Regazzoni	8:44.8 (8)	R, 17 laps, accident
312 PB 0886	3	Peterson/Schenken	7:56.1 (1)	1st, 44 laps
312 PB 0890	2	Redman/Merzario	8:28.1 (6)	2nd, 44 laps
Österreichring 1000-Km (A), 25 June 1972				
312 PB 0884	4	Merzario/Munari	1:42.64 (6)	4th, 164 laps
312 PB 0888	1	Ickx/Redman	1:41.67 (3)	1st, 170 laps; fastest lap, 1:41.88
312 PB 0894	2	Peterson/Schenken	1:42.02 (4)	3rd, 166 laps
312 PB 0896	3	Pace/Marko	1:42.18 (5)	2nd, 169 laps
Watkins Glen 6-Hours (USA), 22 July 1972				
312 PB 0892	87	Redman/Merzario	1:48.84 (4)	R, 136 laps, engine
312 PB 0894	86	Peterson/Schenken	1:47.38 (1)	2nd, 195 laps
312 PB 0896	85	Ickx/Andretti	1:47.86 (2)	1st, 195 laps; fastest lap, 1:47.20
Imola (I), 17 September 1972 (non-championship, preliminary heat/final)				
312 PB 0884	2	Merzario	1:45.53 (3)	1st, 30 laps / 1st, 40 laps; fastest lap, 1:40.1
312 PB 0890	1	Ickx	1:42.25 (1)	8th, 25 laps / 2nd, 40 laps
Kyalami 9-Hours (ZA), 4 November 1972 (non-championship)				
312 PB 0890	1	Ickx/Redman	— (2)	R, 174 laps, engine; fastest lap, 1:22.8
312 PB 0894	2	Regazzoni/Merzario	1:20.3 (1)	1st, 365 laps
Vallelunga 6-Hours (I), 25 March 1973				
312 PB 0888	1	Ickx/Redman	1:10.02 (2)	3rd, 289 laps
312 PB 0892	2	Merzario/Pace	1:10.28 (4)	4th, 289 laps
312 PB 0894	3	Schenken/Reutemann	1:10.82 (5)	2nd, 290 laps; fastest lap, 1:09.7
Dijon 1000-Km (F), 15 April 1973				
312 PB 0890	4	Merzario/Pace	1:01.0 (4)	4th, 308 laps
312 PB 0892	3	Ickx/Redman	1:01.0 (5)	2nd, 312 laps

CHASSIS	NO.	DRIVER(S)	PRACTICE TIME (QUAL. POS.)	RESULT
Monza 1000-Km (I), 25 April 1973				
312 PB 0888	1	Ickx/Redman	1:21.80 (2)	1st, 174 laps
312 PB 0894	3	Schenken/Reutemann	1:22.65 (4)	2nd, 171 laps
312 PB 0896	2	Merzario/Pace	1:22.67 (5)	R, 7 laps, gearbox
Spa-Francorchamps 1000-Km (B), 6 May 1973				
312 PB 0888	1	Ickx/Redman	3:12.7 (1)	R, 37 laps, oil leak
312 PB 0896	2	Merzario/Pace	3:15.4 (3)	4th, 67 laps
Targa Florio (I), 13 May 1973				
312 PB 0892	3	Merzario/Vaccarella	33:38.5 (1)	R, 3 laps, driveshaft
312 PB 0894	5	Ickx/Redman	34:59.1 (4)	R, 3 laps, accident
Nürburgring 1000-Km (D), 27 May 1973				
312 PB 0888	1	Ickx/Redman	7:15.5 (2)	1st, 44 laps
312 PB 0890	2	Merzario/Pace	7:21.7 (5)	2nd, 44 laps
Le Mans 24-Hours (F), 9-10 June 1973				
312 PB 0888	15	Ickx/Redman	3:38.5 (2)	R, 23 hours, engine
312 PB 0892	17	Schenken/Reutemann	3:42.3 (5)	R, 11 hours, engine
312 PB 0896	16	Merzario/Pace	3:37.5 (1)	2nd, 349 laps
Österreichring 1000-Km (A), 24 June 1973				
312 PB 0890	2	Merzario/Pace	1:39.98 (5)	6th, 164 laps
312 PB 0896	1	Ickx/Redman	1:39.64 (3)	3rd, 169 laps
Watkins Glen 6-Hours (USA), 21 July 1973				
312 PB 0890	11	Merzario/Pace	1:44.201 (3)	3rd, 196 laps
312 PB 0892	12	Schenken/Reutemann	1:44.798 (4)	R, 188 laps, distributor
312 PB 0896	10	Ickx/Redman	1:45.469 (5)	2nd, 197 laps

365 GT/BB / BB 512

CHASSIS	NO.	DRIVER(S)	PRACTICE TIME (QUAL. POS.)	RESULT
Daytona 24-Hours (USA), 1-2 February 1975				
365 GT/BB 18095	1	Ballot-Lena/Cudini (NART)	—	R, 1 lap
Sebring 12-Hours (USA), 22 March 1975				
365 GT/BB 18095	111	Minter (NART)	—	6th
Lime Rock (USA), 3 May 1975				
365 GT/BB 18095	5	Minter (NART)	—	R
Road Atlanta (USA), 6 July 1975				
365 GT/BB 18095	5	Minter (NART)	—	Non-starter
Le Mans 24-Hours (F), 11-12 June 1977				
365 GT/BB 18095	75	Migault/Guitteny (NART)	—	16th, 268 laps
Daytona 24-Hours (USA), 4-5 February 1978				
365 GT/BB 18095	5	Migault/Guitteny (NART)	—	22nd
Le Mans 24-Hours (F), 10-11 June 1978				
365 GT/BB 18095*	86	Migault/Guitteny (NART)	—	16th, 262 laps
BB 512	85	Beurlys/Pilette (Beurlys)	—	R, 4 hours, transmission
BB 512	87	Young/Delaunay/Guerin (Chinetti)	—	R, 19 hours
BB 512	88	Andruet/Dini (Pozzi)	—	R, 21 hours
BB 512	89	Ballot-Lena/Lafosse (Pozzi)	—	R, 17 hours

*512 engine

CHASSIS	NO.	DRIVER(S)	PRACTICE TIME (QUAL. POS.)	RESULT
Watkins Glen 6-Hours (USA), 8 July 1978				
365 GT/BB 18095*	25	Migault/Guitteny (NART)	—	11th, 124 laps
*512 engine				
Daytona 24-Hours (USA), 3-4 February 1979				
BB 512 LM/79 Silhouette 26681	66	Andruet/Dini (Pozzi)	1:58.78 (15)	R, withdrawn
BB 512 LM/79 Silhouette 26685	67	Ballot-Lena/Leclére (Pozzi)	1:57.32 (13)	R, withdrawn
BB 512 LM/79 Silhouette 26683	68	Tullius/Bedard/Delaunay (NART)	1:58.82 (16)	R, 6 hours, accident
Le Mans 24-hours (F), 9-10 June 1979				
BB 512 LM/79 Silhouette 27577	61	Beurlys/Faure/O'Rourke/ De Dryver (Beurlys)	4:26.53 (45)	12th, 268 laps
BB 512 LM/79 Silhouette 26681	62	Andruet/Dini (Pozzi)	4:06.64 (30)	R, 19 hours, engine
BB 512 LM/79 Silhouette 26685	63	Leclére/Ballot-Lena/Gregg (Pozzi)	4:00.78 (28)	R, 18 hours, accident
BB 512 LM/79 Silhouette 26683	64	Delaunay/Grandet/Henn (NART)	4:11.47 (36)	R, 4 hours, accident
Daytona 24-Hours (USA), 2-3 February 1980				
BB 512 LM/79 Silhouette 26683	69	Dieudonné/Henn (NART)	1:59.403	R, 14 hours, fuel tank
Le Mans 24-Hours (F), 14-15 June 1980				
BB 512 LM/79 Silhouette	74	Delaunay/Henn (Chinetti)	4:16.6 (50)	R
BB 512 LM/79 Silhouette	78	O'Rourke/Down/Phillips (Rosso)	4:19.7 (60)*	23rd, 261 laps
BB 512 LM/80 Silhouette	75	Guitteny/Bleynie/Libert (Pozzi)	4:11.1 (36)	R
BB 512 LM/80 Silhouette	76	Dieudonné/Xhenceval/Regout (Pozzi)	4:02.6 (24)	10th, 312 laps
BB 512 LM/80 Silhouette	77	Ballot-Lena/Andruet/Dieudonné (Pozzi)	3:58.4 (17)	R
BB 512 LM/80 Silhouette	79	Dini/Violati/Micangeli (Bellancauto)	4:14.3 (41)	R
*Qualified 61st, started as first alternate				
Daytona 24-Hours (USA), 31 January-1 February 1981				
BB 512 LM/80 Silhouette 34445	65	Adamowicz/Knoop (Prancing Horse Farms)	— (23)	R, 579 laps, accident

No.	Type	Built	Raced	Notes
FORMULA 1				
001	312 B	1969	1970-71	Won Österreichring St. Jovite and Mexico City 1970. Current owner Jacky Ickx.
002	312 B	1970	1970-71	Won Kyalami and Ontario 1971. Current owner Schlumpf Museum.
003	312 B	1970	1970-71	Won Hockenheim 1971. Current owner Tom Wheatcroft.
004	312 B	1970	1970-71	Won Monza 1970. Current owner Luigi Chinetti.
005	312 B2	1970	1971-73	Won Brands Hatch 1971 and Nürburgring 1972 Current owner Jacky Ickx.
006	312 B2	1971	1971-73	Won Zandvoort 1971. Current owner SEFAC.
007	312 B2	1971	1971-72	Current owner Pierre Bardinon.
008	312 B2	1972	1972-73	Current owner SEFAC.
009	312 B3	1972	—	*Spazzaneve.* Never raced. Current owner Anthony Bamford.
010	312 B3/B3 S	1973	1973-74	Current owner Anthony Bamford.
011	312 B3/B3 S	1973	1973-74	Current owner Italya Trading Co.
012	312 B3	1973	1973-75	Current owner Ronnie Hoare.
013	—	—	—	Not built.
014	312 B3	1974	1974-75	Current owner William Gelles. Restored at Sport Auto, Modena.
015	312 B3	1974	1974	Won Jarama and Zandvoort 1974. Current owner Stephen Barney.
016	312 B3	1974	1974	Won Nürburgring 1974. Current owner SEFAC.
017	—	—	—	Not built.
018	312 T	1974	1975	Current owner Kroymans B.V. Restored at Sport Auto.
019	312 B3	1974	—	Never raced. Damaged in testing and broken up.
020	312 B3	1974	1975	Current owner SEFAC.
021	312 T	1975	1975	Won Dijon 1975. Current owner SEFAC. Restored at Sport Auto.
022	312 T	1975	1975-76	Won Silverstone and Paul Ricard 1975. Current owner SEFAC. Restored at Sport Auto.
023	312 T/T2	1975	1975-76	Most successful of Formula 1 Ferrari chassis; won Monte Carlo, Zolder, Anderstorp, Watkins Glen 1975, Interlagos and Kyalami 1976. Current owner SEFAC.
024	312 T	1975	1975-76	Won Monza 1975 and Long Beach 1976. Current owner Harley Cluxton.
025	312 T2	1975	1976	Prototype with De Dion rear suspension, converted to standard specification in 1976. Current owner SEFAC.
026	312 T2	1976	1976-77	Won Zolder and Monte Carlo 1976. Current owner Louis Sellyei.
027	312 T2	1976	1976-78	Current owner SEFAC.
028	312 T2	1976	1976	Won Brands Hatch 1976. Destroyed at Nürburgring 1976; new chassis built with same number. Current owner SEFAC.

No.	Type	Built	Raced	Notes
029	312 T2	1976	1977-78	Won Interlagos 1977. Current owner SEFAC.
030	312 T2	1977	1977	Won Kyalami and Zandvoort 1977. Destroyed at Fuji 1977.
031	312 T2	1977	1977-78	Won Hockenheim 1977 and Rio 1978. Current owner Colin Bach.
032	312 T3	1977	1978	Won Long Beach 1978. Current owner SEFAC.
033	312 T3	1978	1978-79	Won Brands Hatch 1978. Current owner SEFAC.
034	312 T3	1978	1978-79	Won Montreal 1978. Current owner SEFAC.
035	312 T3	1978	1978-79	Won Watkins Glen 1978. Current owner SEFAC.
036	312 T3	1978	1978-79	Current owner SEFAC.
037	312 T4/T4 B	1979	1979	Won Kyalami and Long Beach 1979. Current owner SEFAC.
038	312 T4/T4 B	1979	1979	Current owner SEFAC.
039	312 T4	1979	1979	Current owner Harley Cluxton.
040	312 T4/T4 B	1979	1979	Won Zolder, Monte Carlo and Monza 1979. Current owner SEFAC.
041	312 T4/T4 B	1979	1979	Won Watkins Glen 1979. Current owner SEFAC.
042	312 T5	1979	1980	Current owner SEFAC.
043	312 T5	1979	1980	Current owner SEFAC.
044	312 T5	1979	1980	Current owner SEFAC.
045	312 T5	1979	1980	Current owner SEFAC.
046	312 T5	1980	1980	Heavily damaged at Imola 1980.
047	—	—	—	Number assigned to first 126 C turbo.
048	312 T5	1980	1980	Heavily damaged at Imola 1980.

049 and subsequent numbers assigned to 126 C.

312 PB SPORT/PROTOTYPE

No.	Type	Built	Raced	Notes
0876	312 PB	1970	1971	Shown to press December 1970.
0878	312 PB	1970	1971	Won Kyalami 1971
0880	312 PB	1970	1971	Current owner Michael Vernon.
0882	312 PB	1971	1972	Won Sebring and Monza 1972. Current owner Harley Cluxton.
0884	312 PB	1971	1971-72	Won Targa Florio and Imola 1972. Current owner Pierre Bardinon.
0886	312 PB	1971	1972	Won Buenos Aires and Nürburgring 1972. Current owner Harley Cluxton.
0888	312 PB	1972	1972-73	Won Daytona, Brands Hatch and Österreichring 1972, Monza and Nürburgring 1973. Current owner Albert Obrist.
0890	312 PB	1972	1971-73	Won Spa 1972. Converted to side oil radiator and central air scoop in 1973. Current owner Harley Cluxton.
0892	312 PB	1972	1972-73	Current owner Clay Regazzoni.
0894	312 PB	1972	1972-73	Won Kyalami 1972. Current owner William Kontes.
0896	312 PB	1972	1972-73	Won Watkins Glen. 1972. Current owner Albert Obrist.

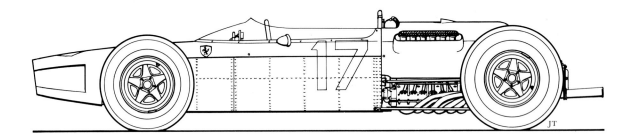

1964 512 F1

Engine: 180-degree horizontally-opposed 12, mounted ahead of and driving rear wheels. Bore 56 mm, stroke 50.4 mm, displacement 1489.6 cc. Seven-main-bearing crankshaft. Aluminum-alloy crankcase/cylinder blocks. Gear-driven twin overhead camshafts for each bank of cylinders, operating one intake and one exhaust valve per cylinder. Lucas indirect fuel injection with two belt-driven pumps. Ignition by four coils and distributor. Single spark plug per cylinder. Compression ratio 9.8:1. Power output 220 bhp at 11,500 rpm. Specific output 147.6 bhp/liter.
Transmission: Dry multi-plate clutch between engine and gearbox. 5-speed and reverse gearbox mounted longitudinally behind engine in unit with final drive.
Chassis: Semi-monocoque with bulkheads, tubing and riveted steel skin, and engine serving as rear chassis member. Formed aluminum upper body panels. Fuel tank capacity 128 liters (33.8 U.S. gallons).
Suspension: Front, upper rocker arms, inboard coil spring/shock absorber units, wide-base lower A-arms, anti-roll bar. Rear, universal-jointed halfshafts, single upper links, reversed lower A-arms, outboard coil spring/shock absorber units, long non-parallel radius rods, anti-roll bar. Dunlop disc brakes, mounted outboard at front and inboard at rear. 15-inch bolt-on cast magnesium-alloy 5-spoke wheels with Dunlop tires, 5.00-15 front and 7.00-15 rear.
Dimensions: Wheelbase 2400 mm (94.5 inches). Track 1350 mm (53.1 inches) front, 1340 mm (52.8 inches) rear. Length 3912 mm (154.0 inches). Width 1629 mm (64.1 inches). Weight, less fuel and driver, 475 kg (1046 pounds). Weight/power ratio 2.16 kg (4.76 pounds)/bhp.

1965 512 F1

As above, except:
Engine: Two spark plugs per cylinder. Power output 225 bhp at 11,500 rpm. Specific output 151.0 bhp/liter.
Dimensions: Length (Monte Carlo short-nose) 3744 mm (147.4 inches). Weight/power ratio 2.11 kg (4.65 pounds)/bhp.

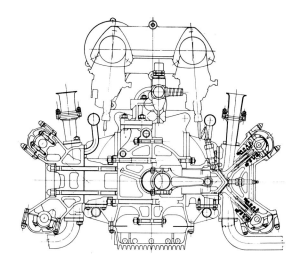

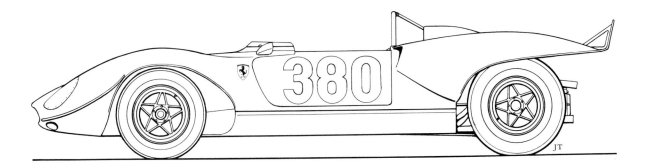

1969 212 E Montagna

Engine: 180-degree horizontally-opposed 12, mounted ahead of and driving rear wheels. Bore 65 mm, stroke 50 mm, displacement 1990.9 cc. Four-main-bearing crankshaft. Aluminum-alloy crankcase/cylinder blocks with cast-iron liners. Gear-driven twin overhead camshafts for each bank of cylinders, operating two intake and two exhaust valves per cylinder. Lucas indirect fuel injection with belt-driven pump. Ignition by Marelli transistor. Single spark plug per cylinder. Compression ratio 11.0:1 (later, 11.3:1). Power output 290 bhp (later, 315-320 bhp) at 11,800 rpm. Specific output 145.6 bhp/liter (later, 160.7 bhp/liter).
Transmission: Dry multi-plate clutch between engine and gearbox. 5-speed and reverse gearbox mounted longitudinally behind engine in unit with final drive.
Chassis: Multi-tubular steel with bulkheads and riveted aluminum skin.

Fiberglass body panels. Fuel capacity 30 liters (7.9 U.S. gallons).
Suspension: Front, unequal-length A-arms, adjustable coil spring/shock absorber units, anti-roll bar. Rear, universal-jointed halfshafts, single upper links, lower A-arms, adjustable outboard coil spring/shock absorber units, long non-parallel radius rods, anti-roll bar. Girling disc brakes, mounted outboard at front and inboard at rear. Bolt-on Campagnolo cast magnesium-alloy 5-spoke wheels, 9.5 x 13-inch front and 14.0 x 13-inch rear, with Firestone tires, 5.00/10.00-13 front and 6.00/14.00-13 rear.
Dimensions: Wheelbase 2340 mm (92.1 inches). Track 1485 mm (58.5 inches) front, 1535 mm (60.4 inches) rear. Length 3800 mm (149.6 inches). Width 1980 mm (77.9 inches). Weight, less fuel and driver, 500 kg (1102 pounds), later 530 kg (1169 pounds). Weight/power ratio 1.72 kg (3.80 pounds)/bhp; later, 1.66 kg (3.65 pounds)/bhp.

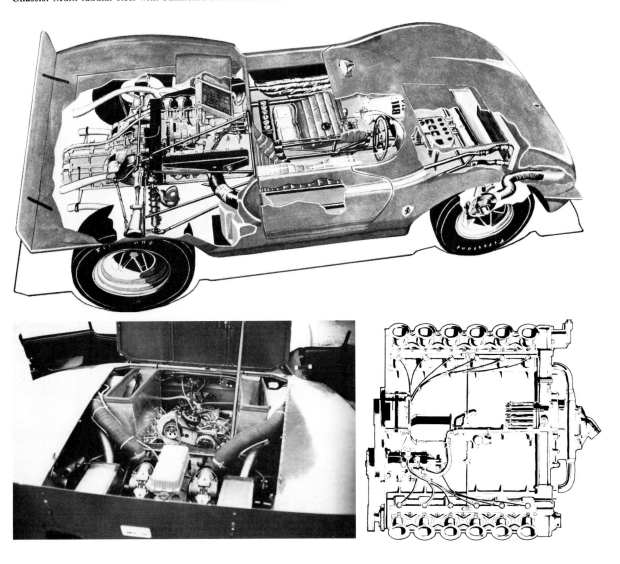

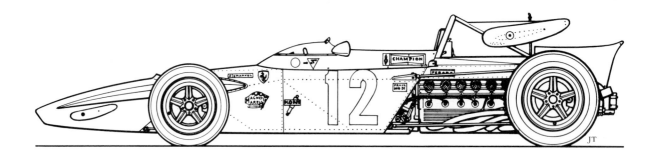

1970 312 B F1

Engine: 180-degree horizontally-opposed 12, mounted ahead of and driving rear wheels. Bore 78.5 mm, stroke 51.5 mm, displacement 2991 cc. Four-main-bearing crankshaft. Aluminum-alloy crankcase/cylinder blocks with cast-iron liners. Gear-driven twin overhead camshafts for each bank of cylinders, operating two intake and two exhaust valves per cylinder. Lucas indirect fuel injection. Ignition by Marelli transistor. Single spark plug per cylinder. Compression ratio 11.8:1. Power output 455 bhp at 11,500 rpm (later, 460 bhp at 11,600 rpm). Specific output 152.1 bhp/liter (later, 153.8 bhp/liter).

Transmission: Dry multi-plate clutch between engine and gearbox. 5-speed and reverse gearbox mounted longitudinally behind engine in unit with final drive.

Chassis: Semi-monocoque with bulkheads, tubing and riveted aluminum skin, and engine suspended from chassis extension. Fiberglass body panels. Fuel tank capacity 200 liters (52.8 U.S. gallons).

Suspension: Front, upper rocker arms, inboard coil spring/shock absorber units, wide-base lower A-arms, anti-roll bar. Rear, universal-jointed halfshafts, single upper links, reversed lower A-arms, outboard coil spring/shock absorber units, long non-parallel radius rods, anti-roll bar. Girling disc brakes, mounted outboard front and rear. Bolt-on Campagnolo cast magnesium-alloy 5-spoke wheels, 13-inch front and 15-inch rear, with Firestone tires, 5.00/10.00-13 front and 12.50/25.00-15 rear.

Dimensions: Wheelbase 2380 mm (93.7 inches). Track 1560 mm (61.4 inches) front, 1570 mm (61.8 inches) rear. Length 3852-3972 mm (151.6-156.3 inches). Width 1887 mm (74.3 inches). Weight, less fuel and driver, 534 kg (1177 pounds). Weight/power ratio 1.17 kg (2.58 pounds)/bhp; later, 1.16 kg (2.56 pounds)/bhp.

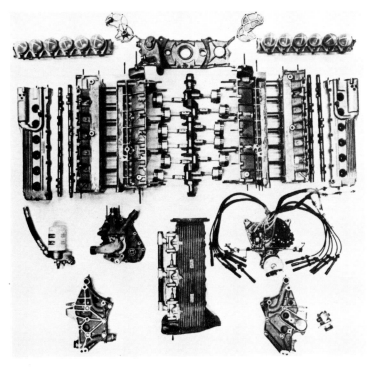

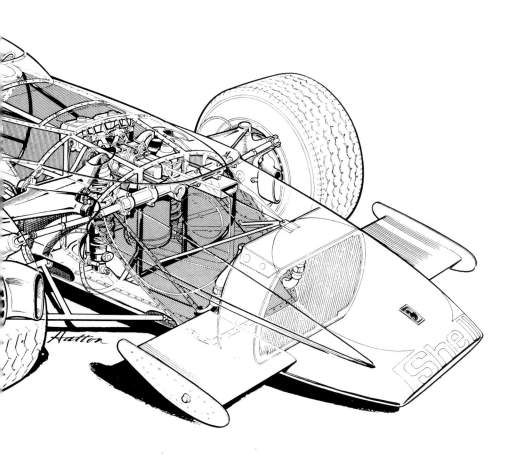

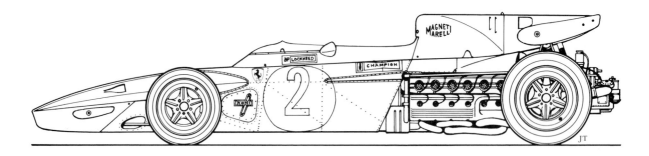

1971 312 B2 F1

Engine: 180-degree horizontally-opposed 12, mounted ahead of and driving rear wheels. Bore 78.5 mm, stroke 51.5 mm, displacement 2991 cc. Four-main-bearing crankshaft. Aluminum-alloy crankcase/cylinder blocks with cast-iron liners. Gear-driven twin overhead camshafts for each bank of cylinders, operating two intake and two exhaust valves per cylinder. Lucas indirect fuel injection. Ignition by Marelli transistor. Single spark plug per cylinder. Compression ratio 11.8:1. Power output 470 bhp at 12,500 rpm. Specific output 157.1 bhp/liter.
Transmission: Dry multi-plate clutch between engine and gearbox. 5-speed and reverse gearbox mounted longitudinally behind engine in unit with final drive.
Chassis: Semi-monocoque with bulkheads, tubing and riveted aluminum skin, and engine suspended from chassis extension. Fiberglass body panels. Fuel tank capacity 220 liters (58.1 U.S. gallons).
Suspension: Front, upper rocker arms, inboard coil spring/shock absorber units, wide-base lower A-arms, anti-roll bar. Rear, universal-jointed halfshafts, reversed upper A-arms with linkage to horizontal inboard coil spring/shock absorber units, lower A-arms, long upper radius rods, anti-roll bar. Lockheed disc brakes, mounted outboard at front and inboard at rear. Bolt-on Campagnolo cast magnesium-alloy 5-spoke wheels, 13-inch front and 13 or 15-inch rear, with Firestone tires, 5.00/10.00-13 front and 13.50/24.00-13 or 12.50/25.00-15 rear.
Dimensions: Wheelbase 2380 mm (93.7 inches). Track 1560 mm (61.4 inches) front, 1570 mm (61.8 inches) rear. Length 3855 mm (151.7 inches). Width 1887-1912 mm (74.3-75.3 inches). Weight, less fuel and driver, 540 kg (1190 pounds). Weight/power ratio 1.15 kg (2.54 pounds)/bhp.

1972 312 B2 F1

As above, except:
Engine: Bore 80 mm, stroke 49.6 mm, displacement 2991.8 cc. Power output 480 bhp at 12,500 rpm. Specific output 160.4 bhp/liter.
Suspension: Rear, single upper links, lower A-arms, outboard coil spring/shock absorber units, long non-parallel radius rods (later, upper rods only), anti-roll bar. Wheels 10.0 x 13-inch front and 16.0 x 13-inch rear.
Dimensions: Wheelbase 2420 mm (96.3 inches). Track 1520 mm (59.8 inches) front, 1580 mm (62.2 inches) rear. Length 4037-4310 mm (158.9-169.7 inches). Width 1922 mm (75.7 inches). Weight, less fuel and driver, 560 kg (1235 pounds). Weight/power ratio 1.17 kg (2.58 pounds)/bhp.

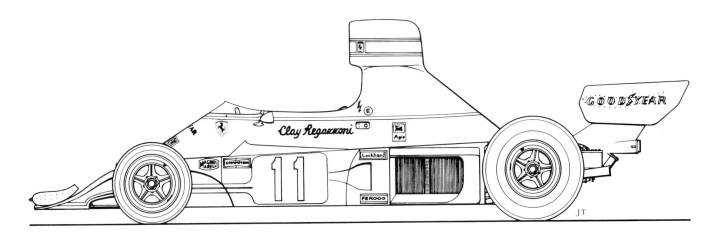

1973 312 B3 F1

Engine: 180-degree horizontally-opposed 12, mounted ahead of and driving rear wheels. Bore 80 mm, stroke 49.6 mm, displacement 2991.8 cc. Four-main-bearing crankshaft. Aluminum-alloy crankcase/cylinder blocks with cast-iron liners. Gear-driven twin overhead camshafts for each bank of cylinders, operating two intake and two exhaust valves per cylinder. Lucas indirect fuel injection. Ignition by Marelli transistor. Single spark plug per cylinder. Compression ratio 11.5:1. Power output 485 bhp at 12,500 rpm. Specific output 162.1 bhp/liter.
Transmission: Dry multi-plate clutch between engine and gearbox. 5-speed and reverse gearbox mounted longitudinally behind engine in unit with final drive.
Chassis: Monocoque. Fiberglass body panels. Side-mounted water radiators ahead of rear wheels (later, single front-mounted radiator in nose). Engine air scoops on each side of body. Fuel tank capacity 195 liters (51.5 U.S. gallons).
Suspension: Front, triangulated upper rocker arms, inboard coil spring/ shock absorber units, wide-base lower A-arms, anti-roll bar. Rear, universal-jointed halfshafts, single upper links, lower A-arms, outboard coil spring/shock absorber units, long upper radius rods, anti-roll bar. Lockheed disc brakes, mounted outboard at front and inboard at rear. Bolt-on Campagnolo cast magnesium-alloy 5-spoke wheels, 10.0 or 11.0 x 13-inch front and 17.0 x 13-inch rear, with Goodyear tires, 9.20/ 20.00-13 front and 14.00/26.00 or 16.20/26.00-13 rear.
Dimensions: Wheelbase 2500 mm (98.4 inches). Track 1620 mm (63.8

inches) front, 1600 mm (63.0 inches) rear. Length 4335-4599 mm (170.7-181.0 inches). Width 2056 mm (80.9 inches). Weight, less fuel and driver, 578 kg (1274 pounds). Weight/power ratio 1.19 kg (2.62 pounds)/bhp.

1973 312 B3 S F1

As above, except:
Chassis: Revised monocoque with water radiators behind front wheels, lateral oil tank and radiator. Engine air scoop above rollbar.
Dimensions: Track 1625 mm (63.9 inches) front, 1606 mm (63.2 inches) rear.

1974 312 B3 F1

As above, except:
Engine: Power output 485 bhp at 12,200 rpm.
Chassis: Further revised monocoque with driving position moved forward, supplementary fuel tank between seat and engine. Vertical engine air scoop, later faired into cockpit cowling.
Suspension: Rear, parallel lower links, long parallel radius rods. Wheels 9.0 or 11.0 x 13-inch front and 16.0 or 18.0 x 13-inch rear.
Dimensions: Wheelbase 2510 mm (98.8 inches). Track 1590 mm (62.6 inches) front, 1620 mm (63.8 inches) rear. Length 4338 mm (170.8 inches). Width 2100 mm (82.7 inches). Weight, less fuel and driver, 590 kg (1301 pounds). Weight/power ratio 1.22 kg (2.69 pounds)/bhp.

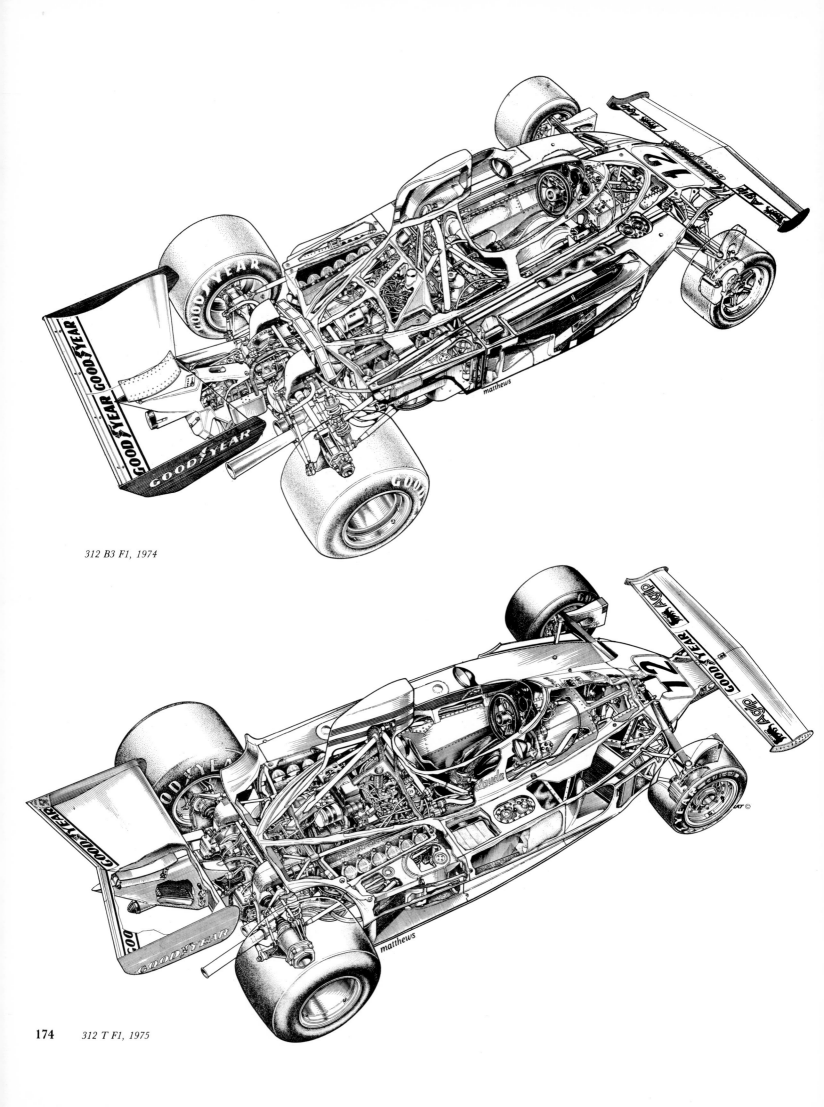

312 B3 F1, 1974

312 T F1, 1975

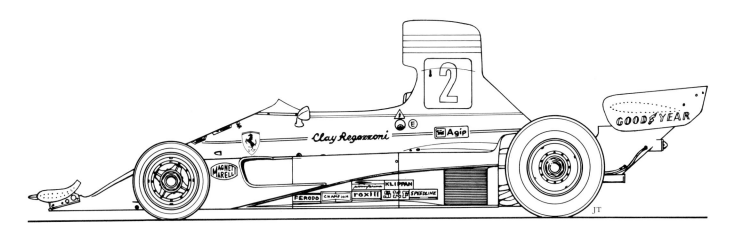

1975 312 T F1

Engine: 180-degree horizontally-opposed 12, mounted ahead of and driving rear wheels. Bore 80 mm, stroke 49.6 mm, displacement 2991.8 cc. Four-main-bearing crankshaft. Aluminum-alloy crankcase/cylinder blocks with cast-iron liners. Gear-driven twin overhead camshafts for each bank of cylinders, operating two intake and two exhaust valves per cylinder. Lucas indirect fuel injection. Ignition by Marelli transistor. Single spark plug per cylinder. Compression ratio 11.5:1. Power output 500 bhp at 12,200 rpm. Specific output 167.1 bhp/liter.
Transmission: Dry multi-plate clutch between engine and gearbox. 5-speed and reverse gearbox mounted transversely behind engine in unit with final drive.
Chassis: Monocoque. Fiberglass body panels. Vertical engine air scoop

faired into cockpit cowling. Fuel tank capacity 195 liters (51.5 U.S. gallons).
Suspension: Front, triangulated upper rocker arms, inboard coil spring/shock absorber units, wide-base lower A-arms, anti-roll bar. Rear, universal-jointed halfshafts, single upper links, reversed lower A-arms, outboard coil spring/shock absorber units, long upper radius rods, anti-roll bar. Lockheed disc brakes, mounted outboard at front and inboard at rear. Center-lock Speedline cast magnesium-alloy wheels, 10.0 or 12.0 x 13-inch 4-spoke front and 16.0, 17.0, 18.0 or 19.0 x 13-inch disc rear, with Goodyear tires, 9.20/20.00-13 front and 16.20/26.00-13 rear.
Dimensions: Wheelbase 2518 mm (99.1 inches). Track 1510 mm (59.4 inches) front, 1530 mm (60.2 inches) rear. Length 4143-4428 mm (163.1-174.3 inches). Width 2030 mm (79.9 inches). Weight, less fuel and driver, 598 kg (1318 pounds). Weight/power ratio 1.19 kg (2.62 pounds)/bhp.

Ing. Forghieri sketch.

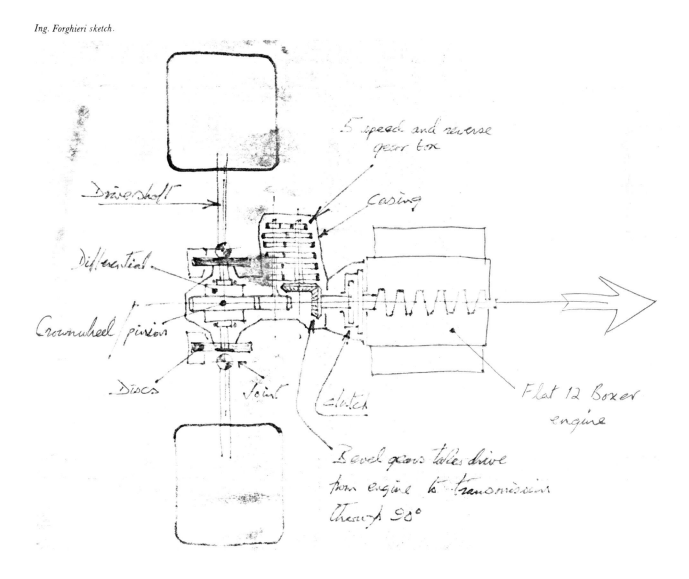

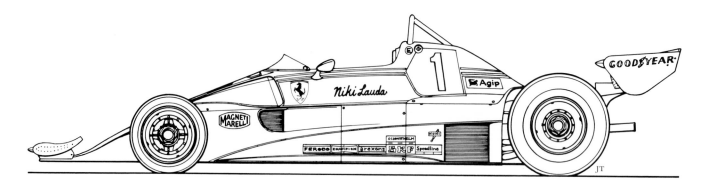

1975 312 T2 F1 (prototype, 025)

As 1975 312 T F1, except:
Chassis: Revised monocoque, more tapered in front with more oblique water radiator mounting. Large lateral NACA-type engine air scoops at front of cockpit cowling.
Suspension: Rear, narrow-base reversed lower A-arms, multi-tubular De Dion structure. Front brakes incorporating aerodynamic air scoops partly covering tires. Wheels 16.0 x 13-inch rear.
Dimensions: Wheelbase 2560 mm (100.8 inches). Track 1400 mm (55.1 inches) front, 1430 mm (56.3 inches) rear. Length 4285 mm (168.5 inches). Width 1836 mm (72.3 inches). Weight, less fuel and driver, 575 kg (1268 pounds). Weight/power ratio 1.15 (2.54 pounds)/bhp.

1976 312 T2 F1

As 1975 312 T F1, except:
Chassis: Revised monocoque, more tapered in front with slightly more oblique water radiator mounting. Large lateral NACA-type engine air scoops at front of cockpit cowling. Fuel tank capacity 210 liters (55.5 U.S. gallons).
Dimensions: Wheelbase 2560 mm (100.8 inches). Track 1450 mm (57.1 inches) rear. Length 4245-4285 mm (166.9-168.5 inches). Width 1933 mm (76.1 inches). Weight, less fuel and driver, 579 kg (1275 pounds). Weight/power ratio 1.16 kg (2.55 pounds)/bhp.

1977 312 T2 F1

As above, except:
Chassis: Small lateral NACA-type air scoops at front of cockpit cowling.
Suspension: Wheels 10.0, 11.0 or 12.0 x 13-inch front and 18.0 or 19.0 x 13-inch rear. Tested experimentally with double 10.0 x 13-inch wheels at rear.
Dimensions: Track 1590 mm (62.6 inches) front, 1560 mm (61.4 inches) rear. Length 4133-4285 mm (162.7-168.5 inches). Width 2043 mm (80.4 inches). With experimental double rear wheels, track 1684 mm (66.3 inches), width 2192 mm (86.3 inches). Weight, less fuel and driver, 575 kg (1268 pounds). Weight/power ratio 1.15 kg (2.54 pounds)/bhp.

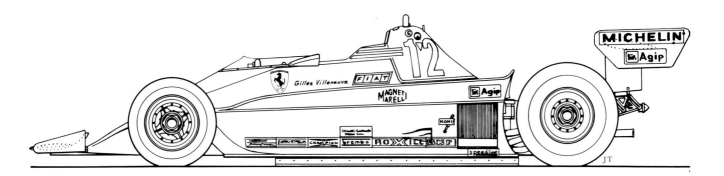

1978 312 T3 F1

Engine: 180-degree horizontally-opposed 12, mounted ahead of and driving rear wheels. Bore 80 mm, stroke 49.6 mm, displacement 2991.8 cc. Four-main-bearing crankshaft. Aluminum-alloy crankcase/cylinder blocks with cast-iron liners. Gear-driven twin overhead camshafts for each bank of cylinders, operating two intake and two exhaust valves per cylinder. Lucas indirect fuel injection. Ignition by Marelli transistor. Single spark plug per cylinder. Compression ratio 11.5:1. Power output 510 bhp at 12,200 rpm. Specific output 170.5 bhp/liter.
Transmission: Dry multi-plate clutch between engine and gearbox. 5-speed and reverse gearbox mounted transversely behind engine in unit with final drive.
Chassis: Monocoque. Fiberglass body panels. Engine air taken in through shallow scoops in front suspension fairings (later, below fairings). Final version raced with sliding skirts in side fairings, between

wheels. Fuel tank capacity 190 liters (50.2 U.S. gallons).
Suspension: Front, triangulated upper rocker arms (reversible right and left for wheelbase change), inboard coil spring/shock absorber units, wide-base lower A-arms, anti-roll bar. Rear, universal-jointed halfshafts, single upper links, reversed lower A-arms, outboard coil spring/shock absorber units, long upper radius rods, anti-roll bar. Lockheed disc brakes, mounted outboard in front and inboard at rear. Center-lock Speedline cast magnesium-alloy wheels, 10.0, 11.0, 12.0 or 13.0 x 13-inch 4-spoke front and 18.0, 19.0, or 20.0 x 13-inch disc rear, with Michelin tires, 24/55-13 (275-13) front and 40/65-13 (450-13) rear.
Dimensions: Wheelbase 2560/2700 mm (100.8/106.3 inches). Track 1620 mm (63.8 inches) front, 1560/1585 mm (61.4/62.4 inches) rear. Length 4250-4332 mm (168.3-170.5 inches). Width 2130 mm (83.8 inches). Weight, less fuel and driver, 595 kg (1312 pounds). Weight/power ratio 1.17 kg (2.57 pounds)/bhp.

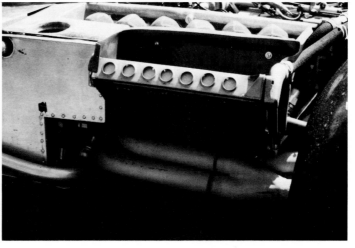

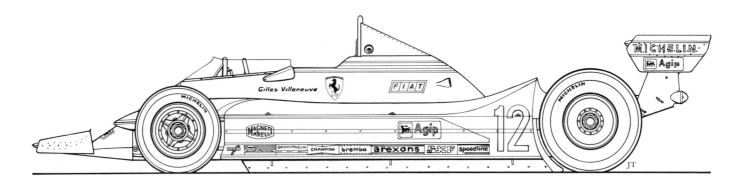

1979 312 T4 F1

Engine: 180-degree horizontally-opposed 12, mounted ahead of and driving rear wheels. Bore 80 mm, stroke 49.6 mm, displacement 2991.8 cc. Four-main-bearing crankshaft. Aluminum-alloy crankcase/cylinder blocks with cast-iron liners. Gear-driven twin overhead camshafts for each bank of cylinders, operating two intake and two exhaust valves per cylinder. Lucas indirect fuel injection. Ignition by Marelli transistor. Single spark plug per cylinder. Compression ratio 11.5:1. Power output 515 bhp at 12,300 rpm. Specific output 172.1 bhp/liter.

Transmission: Dry multi-plate clutch between engine and gearbox. 5-speed and reverse gearbox mounted transversely behind engine in unit with final drive. Tested experimentally with button-operated electro-hydraulic clutch disengagement mechanism.

Chassis: Monocoque. Fiberglass body panels. Side fairings giving aerodynamic downforce, with leading edge ahead of front suspension and engine air taken in below. Sliding skirts in side fairings, between wheels. Fuel tank capacity 185 liters (48.9 U.S. gallons).

Suspension: Front, upper rocker arms, inboard coil spring/shock absorber units, wide-base lower A-arms, anti-roll bar. Rear, universal-jointed halfshafts, upper links with rocker arms operating inboard coil spring/shock absorber units, wide-base lower A-arms, anti-roll bar. Front and rear suspension interconnected by adjustable cables. Lockheed disc brakes, mounted outboard at front and inboard at rear (later T4B, out-board front and rear). Center-lock Speedline cast magnesium-alloy wheels, 11.0, 12.0 or 13.0 x 13-inch 4-spoke front and 18.0 or 19.0 x 13-inch disc rear, with Michelin tires, 23/59-13 (285-13) front and 38/68-13 (460-13) rear.

Dimensions: Wheelbase 2700 mm (106.3 inches). Track 1700 mm (66.9 inches) front, 1600 mm (62.9 inches) rear. Length 4460 mm (175.5 inches). Width 2120 mm (83.4 inches). Weight, less fuel and driver, 590 kg (1301 pounds). Weight/power ratio 1.15 kg (2.52 pounds)/bhp.

1980 312 T5 F1

As 1979 312 T4, except:

Engine: Revised cylinder heads and valve gear, reducing engine width by 44 mm (1.7 inches).

Transmission: 5 or 6-speed and reverse gearbox, in new case.

Chassis: Modified side fairings, with revised air flow through water and oil radiators. Minor body revisions, including central spine behind cockpit cowling.

Suspension: Center-lock Speedline cast magnesium-alloy wheels, slotted disc front and rear. Brakes mounted outboard front and rear.

Dimensions: Track 1700-1751 mm (66.9-68.9 inches) front, 1600-1625 mm (62.9-63.9 inches) rear. Length 4530 mm (178.3 inches). Width 2120-2145 mm (83.4-84.4 inches). Weight, less fuel and driver, 595 kg (1312 pounds). Weight/power ratio 1.16 kg (2.55 pounds)/bhp.

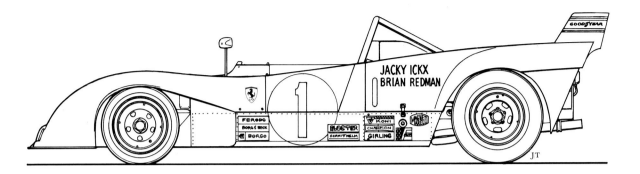

1971 312 PB Sport/Prototype

Engine: 180-degree horizontally-opposed 12, mounted ahead of and driving rear wheels. Bore 78.5 mm, stroke 51.5 mm, displacement 2991 cc. Four-main-bearing crankshaft. Aluminum-alloy crankcase/cylinder blocks with cast-iron liners. Gear-driven twin overhead camshafts for each bank of cylinders, operating two intake and two exhaust valves per cylinder. Lucas indirect fuel injection. Ignition by Marelli transistor. Single spark plug per cylinder. Compression ratio 11.5:1. Power output 440 bhp at 10,800 rpm. Specific output 147.1 bhp/liter.
Transmission: Dry multi-plate clutch between engine and gearbox. 5-speed and reverse gearbox mounted longitudinally behind engine in unit with final drive.
Chassis: Semi-monocoque with bulkheads, tubing and riveted aluminum skin. Fiberglass body panels. 2-seat bodywork with opening for driver only. Fuel tank capacity 120 liters (31.5 U.S. gallons) in single tank.
Suspension: Front, upper A-arms, coil spring/shock absorber units, wide-base lower A-arms, anti-roll bar. Rear, universal-jointed halfshafts, single upper links, lower A-arms, coil spring/shock absorber units, long parallel radius rods, anti-roll bar. Girling disc brakes, mounted outboard front and rear. Center-lock Campagnolo cast magnesium-alloy slotted disc wheels, 13-inch front and rear, with Firestone tires, 5.00/10.00-13 front and 13.50/24.00-13 rear.
Dimensions: Wheelbase 2220 mm (87.4 inches). Track 1560 mm (61.4 inches) front, 1570 mm (61.8 inches) rear. Length 3770 mm (148.4 inches). Width 1960 mm (77.1 inches). Weight, less fuel and driver, 585 kg (1290 pounds). Weight/power ratio 1.33 kg (2.93 pounds)/bhp.

1972 312 PB Sport/Prototype

As 1971 312 PB, except:
Engine: Bore 80 mm, stroke 49.6 mm, displacement 2991.8 cc. Power output 450 bhp at 11,000 rpm. Specific output 150.4 bhp/liter.
Chassis: 2-seat bodywork with headlights and wider cockpit opening for driver and passenger. Full-width rear wing added later. Fuel tank capacity 122 liters (39.9 U.S. gallons) in two tanks.
Suspension: Girling disc brakes, mounted outboard at front and outboard or inboard at rear. Center-lock Campagnolo slotted disc wheels, 13-inch front and 13 or 15-inch rear.
Dimensions: Weight, less fuel and driver, 655 kg (1441 pounds).

1973 312 PB Sport/Prototype

As 1972 312 PB, except:
Engine: Power output 460 bhp at 11,000 rpm (Le Mans version limited to 10,500 rpm and 450 bhp). Specific output 153.7 bhp/liter.
Chassis: Number 0890 had oil radiator mounted on right side, with central scoop for engine air. Le Mans cars had revised bodywork with longer tails and additional headlights.
Suspension: Center-lock Campagnolo slotted disc wheels, 11.0 x 13-inch front and 17.0 x 13-inch or 15-inch rear, with Goodyear tires, 9.00/20.00-13 front and 14.00/24.00-13 or 15 rear.
Dimensions: Wheelbase 2380 mm (92.1 inches). Track 1425 mm (56.1 inches) front, 1448 mm (57.0 inches) rear. Length 3890 mm (153.1 inches). Width 1960 mm (77.1 inches).

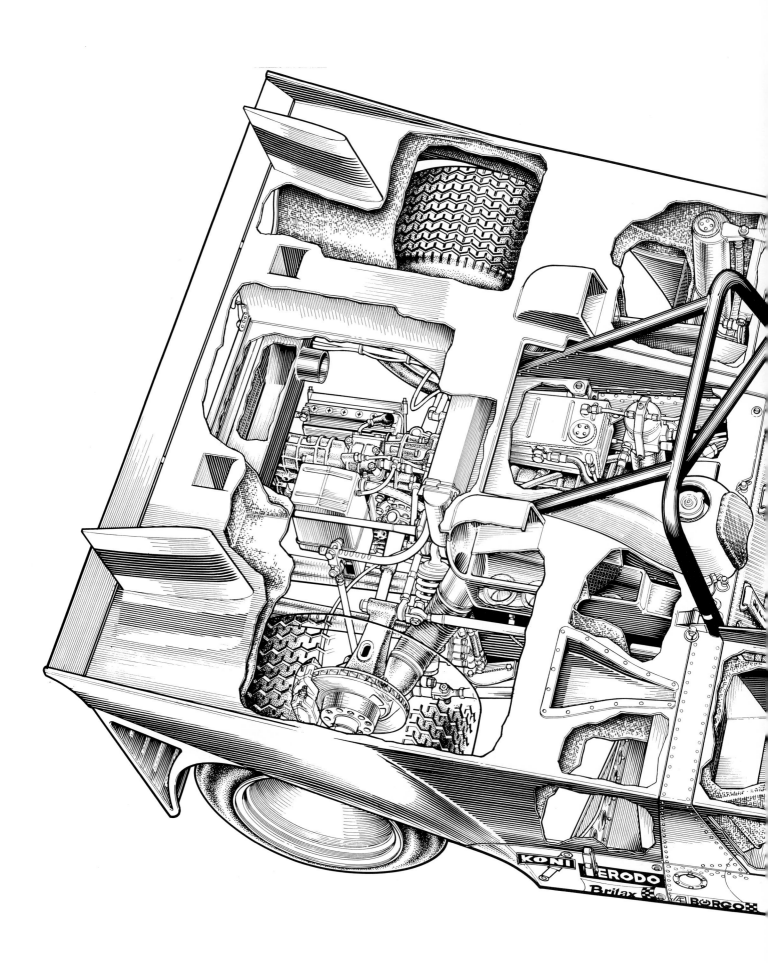

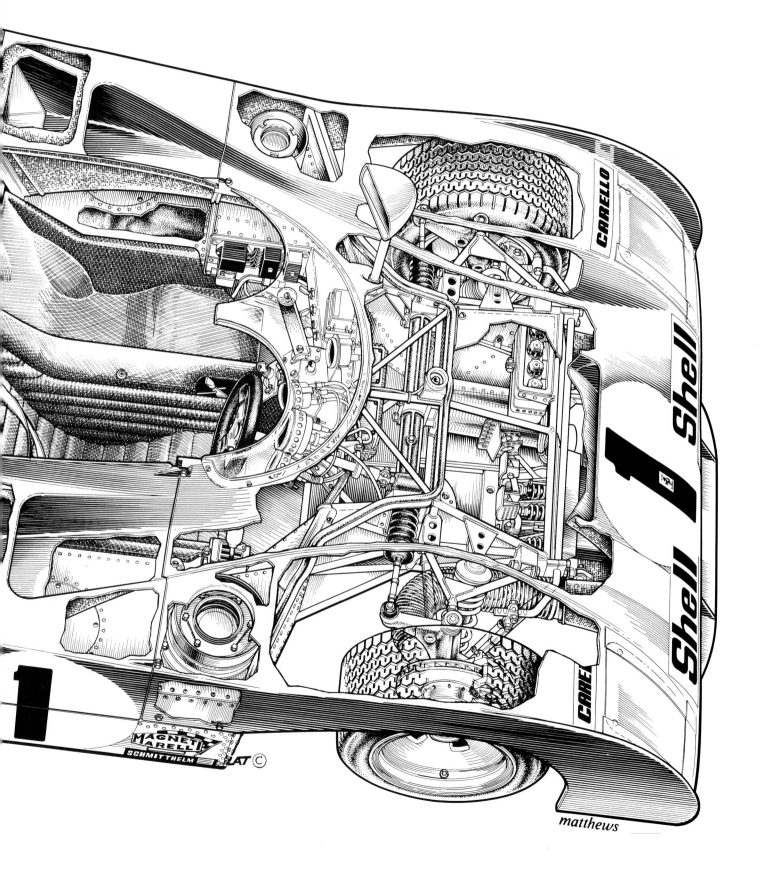

matthews

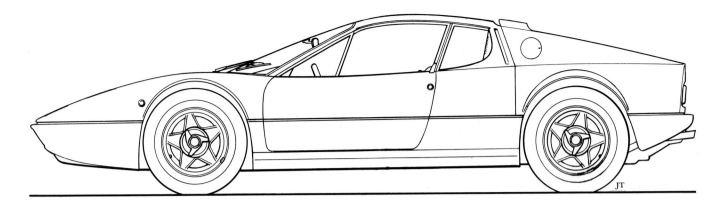

1972-76 365 GT/BB Berlinetta Boxer

Engine: 180-degree horizontally-opposed 12, mounted ahead of and driving rear wheels. Bore 81 mm, stroke 71 mm, displacement 4390 cc. Seven-main-bearing crankshaft. Aluminum-alloy crankcase/cylinder blocks. Belt-driven twin overhead camshafts for each bank of cylinders, operating one intake and one exhaust valve per cylinder. Four triple-throat downdraft Weber 40 IF3C carburetors. Marelli electronic ignition. Single spark plug per cylinder. Twin electric fuel pumps. Dry-sump lubrication, with gear-driven oil pump and separate tank, capacity 13 liters (13.7 quarts). Compression ratio 8.8:1. Power output 380 bhp (production cars probably 360 bhp) at 7200 rpm. Specific output 86.5 bhp/liter (production 82.0 bhp/liter). Torque 40 kg/m (302 lb/ft) at 3900 rpm.

Transmission: Double-plate dry clutch, hydraulically-operated, at rear of engine. 5-speed and reverse all-synchronized gearbox mounted below engine. Limited-slip differential incorporated in final-drive unit. Final-drive ratio 13/45 (3.46:1). Gear ratios 2.64, 1.89, 1.43, 1.08 and 0.82:1.

Chassis: Tubular frame with bulkheads and separate steel and aluminum body. Fuel tank capacity 120 liters (31.5 U.S. gallons) in two tanks.

Suspension: Front, upper and lower A-arms, coil spring/shock absorber units, anti-roll bar. Rear, universal-jointed halfshafts, upper and lower A-arms, double coil spring/shock absorber units, anti-roll bar. Ventilated disc brakes, operated by hydraulic pump and coaxial plungers; two separate circuits, pneumatic brake booster and vacuum pump. Center-lock Cromodora cast light-alloy 5-spoke wheels, 7.5 x 15-inch front and 9.0 x 15-inch rear, with Michelin tires, 215/70 VR-15 front and rear. Spare tire 105 R 20X.

Dimensions: Wheelbase 2500 mm (98.4 inches). Track 1500 mm (59.0 inches) front, 1520 mm (59.8 inches) rear. Length 4360 mm (171.6 inches). Width 1800 mm (70.9 inches). Height 1120 mm (44.1 inches). Curb weight 1120 kg (2469 pounds) prototype; production models up to 200 kg greater and U.S. versions even heavier. Weight/power ratio 2.94 kg (6.49 pounds)/bhp; production 3.66 kg (7.09 pounds)/bhp.

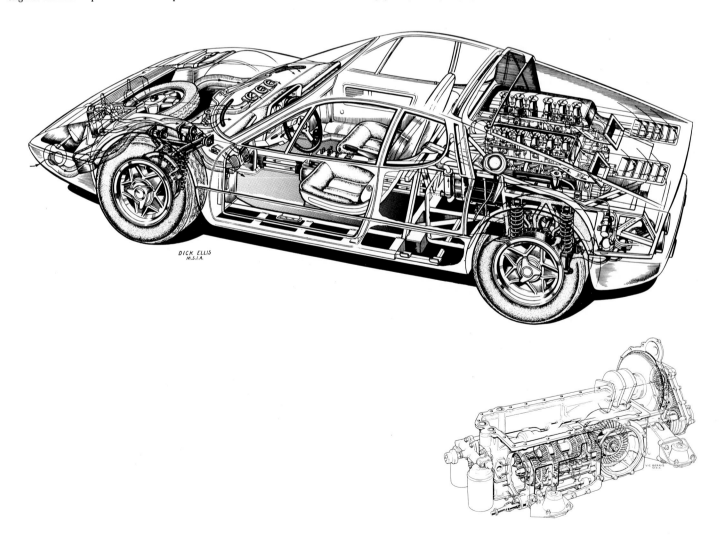

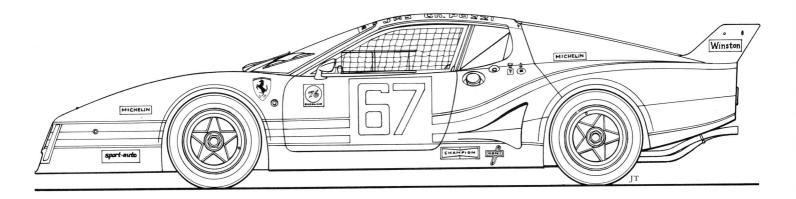

1976-81 BB 512 Berlinetta Boxer

As 1972 365 GT/BB, except:

Engine: Bore 82 mm, stroke 78 mm, displacement 4942 cc. Compression ratio 9.2:1. Power output 360 bhp at 6200 rpm. Specific output 72.8 bhp/liter. Torque 46 kg/m (343 lb/ft) at 4600 rpm.

Transmission: Final-drive ratio 14/45 (3.21:1). Gear ratios 2.94, 2.09, 1.59, 1.20 and 0.91:1.

Chassis: Front air dam. NACA-type air scoops in rocker panels for oil coolers. Revised louvers on rear deck.

Suspension: Tires 225/70 VR-15 rear.

Dimensions: Track 1563 mm (61.5 inches) rear. Length 4400 mm (173.2 inches). Width 1830 mm (72.0 inches). Weight 1400 kg (3088 pounds); U.S. versions heavier. Weight/power ratio 3.88 kg (8.58 pounds)/bhp.

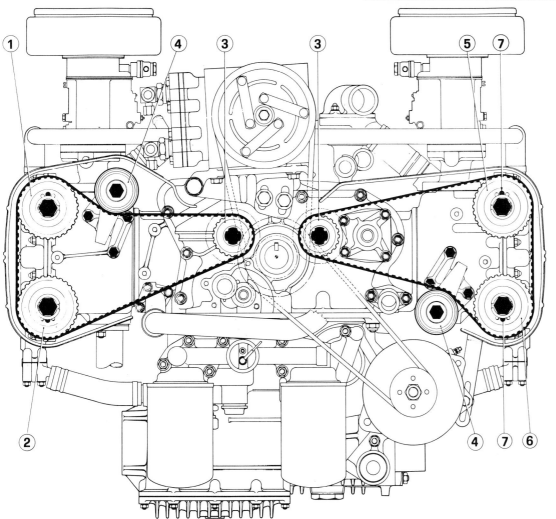

Acknowledgements

Photographs by
Jesse Alexander / Giorgio Bellia / Lionel Birnbom
John Blakemore / Don Bok / Gerhart Brinkmann
Peter Coltrin / Richard Corson / Bob Costanzo
Jutta Fausel / Ferrari SpA SEFAC / Bill Fox
Gaspare Galante / Mike Geissinger / Geoffrey Goddard
Ron Hussey / Jeff Hutchinson / Ed Ikuta / Hiroshi Kitsune
John Lamm / London Art Tech / Jean-Francois Marchet
Mike Meyer / William A. Motta / Bill Oursler
Paul Pappalardo / Alain Petitpierre / Phipps Photographic
Carrozzeria Pininfarina / Rainer Schlegelmilch
Alessandro Stefanini / James Taylor / Jonathan Thompson
Bob Tronolone / Chris Van Wyk / Franco Villani
Renardo Volpi / Bill Warner

Drawings by
Vic Berris / Dick Ellis / Ferrari SpA SEFAC
Brian Hatton / London Art Tech / Tony Matthews
Carrozzeria Pininfarina / Jonathan Thompson

Book design by Jonathan Thompson

Additional material and assistance was generously
provided by Dean Batchelor, Rob de la Rive Box, Harley
Cluxton, Bob Donner, Paul Harsanyi, Junichiro Hiramatsu,
Michael Lynch, Ellida Maki, Scott Malcolm, Ed Niles, Gene Parrill,
Antoine Prunet, Chuck Queener, Gerald Roush, Joe Rusz,
Michael Sheehan, Wilhelmina Sheehan, Chuck Smith,
Spencer Stillman, Kevin Thompson and Walt Woron.